CHRISTIANITY
UNSHACKLED

CHRISTIANITY
UNSHACKLED

ARE YOU A TRUTH SEEKER?

Harold R. Eberle

DESTINY IMAGE® PUBLISHERS, INC.
P.O. Box 310, Shippensburg, PA 17257-0310

"Speaking to the Purposes of God for This Generation and for the Generations to Come."

This book and all other Destiny Image, Revival Press, MercyPlace, Fresh Bread, Destiny Image Fiction, and Treasure House books are available at Christian bookstores and distributors worldwide.

Previously published by Worldcast Publishing as *Christianity Unshackled–Christianity Separate from the Western Worldview.*

For a U.S. bookstore nearest you, call 1-800-722-6774.
For more information on foreign distributors, call 717-532-3040.
Or reach us on the Internet: www.destinyimage.com

ISBN 10: 0-7684-3141-7   ISBN 13: 978-0-7684-3141-4

For Worldwide Distribution, Printed in the U.S.A.

1 2 3 4 5 6 7 8 9 10 11 / 14 13 12 11 10 09

CREDITS AND THANKS

I didn't know I had so many smart friends until I asked them to edit my book. Each of them—competent in their own fields—read through and added suggestions. They wouldn't let me get away with any careless or unresearched remarks. Among those who helped are Andy Briesmeister, Carol Keir, Ted and Paula Mangini, Leon Kemp, Delores Topliff, John Garfield, Sarah Swan, Matthew Cook, and Ian Strader. James Bryson deserves special mention as he has been my writing coach through many projects such as this. Thanks to all of you.

The staff of Destiny Image have helped tremendously. Johnathan I. Nori and Tracy Shuman demonstrated remarkable patience with me as they tried to improve this "baby" of which I was over protective. God bless you and your ministry.

Even though so many people have added their insights and corrections, remaining errors, along with the basic position of this book, are my own responsibility.

Endorsements

Christianity Unshackled, written by my friend Harold Eberle, is a refreshing read. To anyone searching for truth in the context of how history shapes our thinking today, this book is for you! I highly recommend this informative and inspiring book to gain a biblical worldview. Thanks, Harold, for this vital contribution to the Kingdom of God in our day.

Larry Kreider
Author and International Director
DOVE Christian Fellowship International (DCFI)

Harold Eberle, more than anyone else I know of, has the ability to explain profound areas of theology, philosophy, history, and apologetics in straightforward, uncomplicated, and understandable language. *Christianity Unshackled* is a history-changing book. If Church leaders across the board would take the time to examine Eberle's thoughts about worldview, digest them, and implement them in real life, the Church as we know it could be radically reformed!

Dr. C. Peter Wagner
Presiding Apostle, International Coalition of Apostles

I have known Harold for over 15 years, and he has always strongly challenged my mind. In *Christianity Unshackled* he dismantles an enormous tangle of thought patterns that are embedded in the modern Church but have nothing to do with Jesus and the heart of God. Many things look good, but we know that there is something wrong. Harold brings those things to light. He makes you think in ways that many believers are afraid of because it takes away their sense of security.

This book is about maturity, freedom, and life. In the end it reveals peace, joy, and righteousness. We know that there is nothing new under the sun, but something can be new for us in a specific moment and time—we call it revelation. This book offers that. It takes away obstacles and sets people free to live a victorious lifestyle in the Kingdom of God.

Dolf de Voogd van der Straaten
Author, *Prophet to the Nations*
Vlissingen, The Netherlands

I have worked with Harold to establish 12 Bible school leadership training centers in Central and Eastern Africa. We have imparted to thousands of leaders in Africa and other parts of the world. I've been blessed to have read many of Harold's books and I am fully persuaded that *Christianity Unshackled* is a must-read for every Christian leader.

In an age when Western thought has infiltrated the Church, this is a book in time to help Church leaders and Christians identify the truths that do not erode the Gospel of its purity and power. Through reading *Christianity Unshackled,* you will be firmly grounded in truth so as not to be tossed back and forth by the winds of doctrinal teachings that are riddled with the wisdom and knowledge of this age.

I recommend and highly endorse *Christianity Unshackled* as a revelation for this hour and an inspirational work of the Holy Spirit that will bring enlightenment, empowerment, and sanctity to the truths of the Word of God.

Harold's previous book, *Victorious Eschatology*, has brought tremendous light on what the Church ought to be expecting in these last days. Now *Christianity Unshackled* offers wisdom on how to bring forth the victory through the revelation and manifestation of the truths of the unadulterated Word of God.

Dr. Weston Gitonga
Director of Destiny Bible Schools, Africa
Senior Presiding Bishop of Jesus Exaltation Faith Ministries International

Harold Eberle is an amazing optimist. In this book he puts forth an optimistic worldview that he defends from the Bible. He is amazingly able to synthesize a lot of important material and put it in clear and simple English. There is much to gain and much challenge to received dogma. Yet his book is refreshing in its challenge. Much of the book restores us to a more Hebraic (might I say, Jewish) rooted understanding of God and the world. This is a worthy read that challenges both those who agree and those who do not to clarify their thinking and prove it is really biblical!

Dr. Daniel Juster
Author of *Jewish Roots* and
Israel, the Church, and the Last Days

TABLE OF CONTENTS

FOREWORD

F OR CENTURIES GOD has been restoring the Church to the place of authority and power that we read of in the Book of Acts. Practices and truths that were lost after the first 100 years are still being restored. These elements of Kingdom lifestyle are being brought back to the forefront through the Holy Spirit's transforming work. A simple study of Church history will bear this out: each movement helps to restore doctrine and its corresponding experience that was thought to exist only in history.

Tragically, it is often those who were at the "spear point" of God's revolutionary movement in the *last* season who become the very ones who resist the needed changes in the *next* one. It is very hard for people to pay a price to be in a great move of God and then watch as another generation rises up to further refine what they gave their lives for. While understandable, it is equally sad.

One of our greatest challenges is to keep "moving with the cloud." The temptation we face is to celebrate all the changes that God has brought about in history but assume that the Church is as it should be. That view usually labels any attempt to bring about further change as the work of the enemy trying to get us off track. While the spirit of darkness will always work to deceive, our biggest problem is within. And that problem often involves our worldview. We don't always see why we think the way we do, nor do we realize the long-term effect of that perspective. But God is faithful to raise up people with wisdom and understanding to help us navigate our way into all that God intended.

Harold Eberle is one such gift to the Church. His sanctified brilliance, coupled with his passion for a more authentic expression of the Gospel, gives him a clear view of the Church through the lens of history to the present and where God is ultimately taking us. While Harold is wonderfully positive in his approach to life, he challenges the things we often take for granted in our thoughts and practices. I, for one, am very thankful for his role in this mounting reformation.

Christianity Unshackled is timely and provocative in all the right ways. I read this manuscript with excitement as I can see that God is about to use Harold once again to challenge accepted norms and bring us into a deeper Kingdom experience. This book probes deeply. Yet it brings great hope, for understanding gives hope. This unusual combination of challenge with hope will take the reader through a journey that will ultimately lead to a more profound sense of God's presence and purpose.

The passion to live and display a more authentic Gospel is becoming the universal cry of the Church. The time has come to joyfully embrace the privilege to give a fuller expression of Jesus on the earth by allowing the Holy Spirit to lead us into much needed change. This book provides an essential key for the next season.

Bill Johnson
Author of *When Heaven Invades Earth* and
Face to Face With God
Senior Pastor of Bethel Church, Redding, CA

INTRODUCTION

W E CHRISTIANS in the Western world like to think that our Christianity has been formed strictly from truths revealed in the Bible. In reality, our thoughts have developed over the course of 2,000 years intertwined with Western thought. As a consequence, our form of Christianity is a Western form of Christianity. When people groups of other cultures embrace Christianity, they develop ideas and beliefs different from our own. They read the same Bible we read, yet they arrive at different conclusions and live differently than we do—often in significant ways.

As long as Christians remain isolated and only associated with people of similar backgrounds, they can cling to the idea that their way of thinking is the only correct way of thinking. But if they expose themselves to how others think, they usually have to reevaluate their own ideas and decide what is truly Christian and what is simply their own culture.

I have been constantly challenged in my own belief system because I have spent the last 24 years working with various Christian communities around the world. In many ways I have found my Western form of Christianity lacking. For example, I find that Christians who live under persecution understand the importance of community in ways my culture cannot comprehend. Christians in developing nations talk frequently about spiritual and supernatural experiences like those recorded in the Bible. And some of our brethren in poverty-stricken areas have an abiding joy that is beyond the grasp of Christians in prosperous regions of the world.

I am not saying that they are right and we are wrong. In many ways our Western Christianity has been tested over the course of centuries and it has withstood the test of time. I maintain that Western Christianity is the most stable and well thought-out in the world. Yet, in some areas we come up short. There are some significant things we can learn from our brothers and sisters around the world.

In my personal wrestling with these issues I have endeavored to understand how our Western form of Christianity developed. Being a student of history, I wanted to answer the question, "How did we get where we are?" To answer this I will dedicate Section I of this book to skimming through Western history to see how the modern Western worldview developed.

What will become evident is how the foundation of our Western thought patterns was laid down in the ancient Greek world. That foundation has a clear demarcation between the spiritual world and the natural world. Unfortunately, Christianity was laid upon that spiritual/natural division when Christianity emerged out of Judaism in the first century. That will be explained in coming pages.

Today most Western people do not realize how profoundly their lives have been influenced by Western thought or the Western worldview. At the very least, the Western worldview leads a person to embrace a form of godliness but to deny the power thereof. At worst, it causes one to deny the existence of God.

Knowing this, I am passionate to help the Church. I cannot bear to see Christians being swallowed up by a system of thought that destroys faith and undermines the authority of the Gospel. I want to shake the Church out of lethargy and launch her into life and victory.

In an attempt to do this, I want to offer a Christian worldview separated from the Western worldview. Therefore, in Section II, I will develop and explain that Christian worldview. I will lay biblical truths on a foundation that sees the spiritual and natural realms as fully integrated rather than as two separate worlds. This will lead us into a clearer understanding of the nature of God, humanity, and the world. These concepts will provide a framework for a Christian worldview—one that is similar to those who wrote the Bible.

In the following pages, I am offering a whole worldview, "a complete package." In earlier books that I have written, I have addressed in greater depth some of the individual subjects that are key to our worldview. As we proceed, I will reference those books in case you are interested in further study on specific topics.

Let me warn you now about the negative observations I will be making concerning some of the great leaders in Church history. In other books I have written, I have spoken very positively, noting some of their great contributions. However, here I am trying to show where Western thought went wrong. It is impossible to point out errors within Western thought without being critical of those who molded those thoughts. I apologize now if I portray any of your favorite Christian heroes too negatively. Like you, I am grateful and indebted to our forefathers who wrestled with theological issues and gave their lives to establish Christian truths throughout the world.

Why You Should Read This Book

Amidst all the above talk about the Western worldview, you may find yourself wondering, *Yes, but what does all this have to do with me? Does any of this really apply to my life?*

Yes! This book will give you a Christian worldview upon which you can solidly build your life and confidently make future decisions. You will have a worldview that will hold up against the most fearsome attacks of atheists. You will clearly see a worldview that answers the questions of today's society. And, perhaps most importantly, you will have a worldview that opens your heart and mind to a God who is willing to walk with you and act on your behalf.

SECTION I

THE DEVELOPMENT OF OUR WESTERN WORLDVIEW

How did we get to where we are? Let's walk through Western history to see how our present thought patterns are the product of those who lived before us.

Chapter 1

THE BIRTH OF WESTERN THOUGHT

WHEN JESUS STEPPED onto the stage of human history, it was into a Jewish family, surrounded by the Greek culture and Roman government. This is the foundation upon which Christianity was built. As we examine this foundation, we will see how it affected (and continues to affect) modern-day Western Christianity.

In Jesus' time, the Greek culture was dominant throughout the Middle East due to the far-reaching Greek Empire, which had extended (circa 334-146 B.C.) from Greece to India. Starting with Alexander the Great, the earliest Greek rulers believed that they could most effectively bring foreign people under their rule by destroying the conquered nation's native culture, including their art, literature, and consciousness of local history. As a result, a tremendous purging of culture took place during that period, and it was accompanied by the imposition of the Greek culture, now called the Hellenization of society.

Pressure to conform was particularly strong upon the Jews living outside of Israel. One result of the Hellenization of Judaism was the need for the Septuagint, a Greek translation of the Jewish Bible. That translation became the most commonly read version of the Old Testament among Jews living outside of their homeland. We can read in the Book of Acts about the "Hellenistic Jews"—called "Grecians" in some translations (see Acts 6:1)—which referred to those Jews who had embraced the language, lifestyle, and culture of the surrounding Greek people.

Around 146 B.C., the Roman Empire (146 B.C.-A.D. 476) began displacing the Greek Empire and then expanded farther into Western Europe and Northern Africa. However, the Roman leaders were not interested in changing the local cultures of the various people groups. They simply demanded governmental control while maintaining much of the already established Greek culture. Romans respected Greek ways, taking on many of their gods and embracing the teachings of some of their great philosophers such as Socrates, Plato, and Aristotle (circa 500-300 B.C.).

This is the world into which Christianity was born. When local persecution and evangelistic efforts caused the early Christians to move out of the Jewish homeland, they came face to face with the Greek culture and Roman government.

In that environment Western thought took shape. Of course, these were not the only influences, as every people group influences those with whom they come in contact. However, it is the general patterns of thought that we will be identifying; and there is no doubt that by the end of the Ancient Period most of Europe had embraced some form of Christianity, yet the foundation of their thoughts was laid by the ancient Greeks.

Development of the Western Worldview During the Ancient Time Period

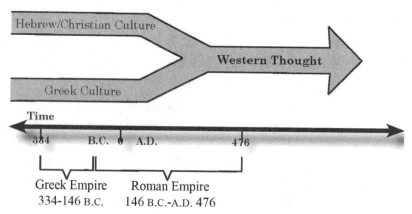

Numerous divergent beliefs developed during the Hellenization of Christianity and Judaism, but one pattern of thought for which we can be thankful is the Greek philosophical manner of questioning everything. It was Socrates who asked so many questions of the people around him that they were left doubting whether they themselves actually knew anything. He was persistent, like a child asking his mother, "Why?" and then following her answer up with another "Why?", and then another "Why?", and on and on.

Like a mother in frustration, the people around Socrates realized that they eventually are forced to admit that they simply do not know the answers to the most basic issues upon which their lives are based. The lesson from this was the realization that only after questioning all assumptions can people develop any sense of confidence that they truly know anything. Such a manner of pursuing truth is a fundamental thought pattern of the Western worldview.

That is a good thing. We will ask questions in the pages to follow. We will challenge our assumptions. We will seek truth.

What we will reject is the ancient Greek way of separating the spiritual world from the natural world (which I will explain in the next chapter). As we trace this thinking pattern from the Ancient Period through the Middle Ages, and then into the Modern Period, we will see that this way of thinking has influenced every nation on earth as Western thought and Western Christianity have spread around the world.

Discussion Questions

1. Why do you think God chose to place the birth of Christianity at the crossroads of Judaism, Greek culture, and Roman government?

2. Following Socrates' example, ask yourself: Why?

3. Then ask yourself *Why?* again.

Chapter 2

THE GREAT DIVIDE IN WESTERN THOUGHT

A NCIENT GREEK PHILOSOPHERS, like Plato and Aristotle, followed in the footsteps of Socrates, spending much time contem-
plating and discussing the nature of things. They observed the natural
world through their senses, but concluded that there must be an invisible, spiritual world lying behind the visible world. All of their thought
patterns and teachings were built on this fundamental idea that there are
two worlds: a natural world and a spiritual world.

However, their understanding of the spiritual world was not the
same as that of modern Christians. The Greek philosophers understood
the invisible world to be the realm of thought and truth. It was not necessarily the world in which God and angels dwell. They saw it as the
world that people access and dwell in through their own thoughts and
contemplation of truth.

Foundation of the Ancient Greek Worldview

Spiritual World: Realm of Thought and Truth
Natural World

This division between the natural world and the spiritual world became the foundation of all education and scholarly discussion throughout the ancient Greek and Roman empires.

A foundation is something upon which a structure is built. If a building is being constructed, its shape and size are determined by the foundation upon which it is erected. It may take years to complete the building, and some variations may be made in construction materials and designs, but the fundamental structure is predetermined by the foundation undergirding the whole building.

Other cultures have a different foundation. For example, a major division that the ancient Chinese had at the foundation of their thoughts was opposing forces called yin and yang. In their minds, every-thing in existence is balanced between these two opposing forces.

An entirely different foundation can be seen in a certain primitive tribe that divided all things into two categories: sharp objects and soft objects. With this as the foundation of their thought patterns, they placed sharp rocks in the same category as animals with sharp spines. In their minds the porcupine was more like a sharp rock than it was like a dog. A soft section of grass was more like a furry rabbit than it was like a tree.

We can imagine many ways those thought patterns would limit people. For example, the tribe that thought in terms of sharp versus soft objects had no category for animals. Since some animals fit in the sharp category and others in the soft category, the people were unable to form in their mind a category for all animals. What is an animal? What is a plant? These questions would have been difficult for them to answer. Further, it would have been very difficult for them to learn a language like English that has entirely different categories.

Every people group has organized their concepts and language into specific patterns and categories. Those patterns have evolved over many generations; hence, they become so much a part of people's culture that they cannot understand the world apart from them. Those patterns form the framework through which people view the world.

What we need to realize is that our own culture has formed categories that both facilitate and limit our understanding of the world around us. Beginning with the ancient Greek philosophers, our Western thought patterns have all been built on the foundation of the spiritual/natural dichotomy. Even today, every field of study is divided accordingly. Whether we talk about sociology, economics, medicine, biology, astronomy, anthropology, philosophy, religion, etc., Western people superimpose all of their thoughts upon the foundation of the spiritual/natural division. As we continue, we will see how this way of thinking profoundly influences everything we do and believe in our modern Western world.

The ancient Greek philosophers not only separated the spiritual from the natural, but they also thought of the spiritual world as more real than the natural world. The natural world was considered a lower realm or even insignificant.

Contrast this ancient Greek pattern of thought with the ancient Hebrew way of thinking (before the Hellenization of Judaism). For the ancient Hebrews, the spiritual and natural dimensions were not distinctly separated. In fact, there was no wall or barrier between the two. The God who exists in the spiritual realm intervenes in the natural realm. Jewish history is filled with events in which God entered and acted in history. Even more importantly, human beings can dialogue with, influence, and know God.

To be accurate, we cannot even refer to the spiritual realm as the spiritual world. According to Hebrew and biblical thought there is only one world. It is the one world that God created. There are both visible (physical) and invisible (spiritual) things in the one world. Within that one world, both the spiritual and the natural realms are real and significant.

27

Foundation of Ancient Hebrew Thought

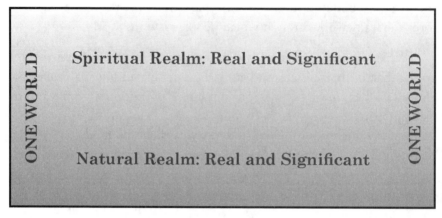

Christianity started as a Jewish sect, and its forebears are the same as those of Judaism. The Old and New Testaments were written from the foundation of the ancient Hebrew worldview. In other words, the Bible was written from the foundation that saw no wall between the spiritual and natural realms.

This reveals the problem facing us. As Christianity was emerging out of Judaism in the first and second centuries, Greek and Roman people tried to understand biblical truths with the spiritual/natural division at the foundation of their thoughts.

Western Christianity Laid on the Ancient Greek Spiritual/Natural Division

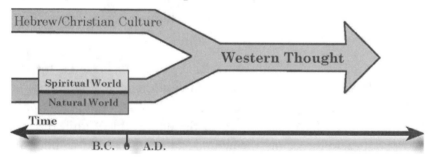

Even today, Western Christians read the Bible through the lens of the spiritual/natural division. The apostle Paul warned that we must accurately divide the Word of God (see 2 Tim. 2:15). If we read the Bible while categorizing and drawing our lines of division in the wrong manner, we may develop ideas and beliefs not originally intended by the Bible authors. Even as Christians we can misunderstand the fundamental truths of our own faith. This will become evident as we continue following the development of the Western worldview.

Discussion Questions

1. Can you think of examples where the Western worldview delineates between the natural world and the spiritual world?

2. Can you think of examples of the opposite: where the natural world and spiritual world are treated as one?

3. What bearing might the Western division of spiritual versus natural have on how we view ourselves?

Chapter 3

First Major Outworking: Gnosticism

JOHN WAS THE APOSTLE known for his missionary work in Asia Minor, one of the regions most profoundly engulfed in Greek thought and culture. Knowing this brings new light to the words with which he started his Gospel:

> *In the beginning was the Word, and the Word was with God, and the Word was God...*(John 1:1).

Educated people in Asia Minor would have understood these words within the Greek worldview. They thought of the spiritual world as the world of thought and truth—or words. When John wrote that *"the Word was God,"* he was introducing into their worldview a personal God who encompasses all thought and truth—One who exists in the spiritual world.

Introducing God Into the Greek Worldview

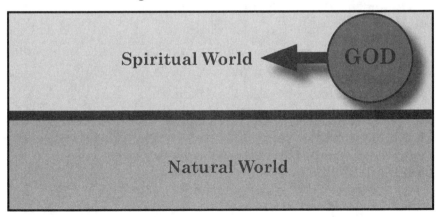

Tens of thousands of Greek-minded people embraced the God preached to them by the early Christians. However, they had a major obstacle in accepting the whole Christian message. They not only saw the natural world as insignificant, but by the end of the first century many of them came to think of the natural world as inferior, even corrupt. As a consequence, they could not understand how a God who exists in the perfect world of thought and truth could have come into this corrupt world. In other words, they could not accept the idea that God came into this world in Jesus.

As a consequence, they developed aberrant understandings of Jesus Christ. Some of them simply denied that Jesus was God. Others said that the spiritual God dwelt in a human being named Jesus. Another group said that Jesus was never really human, but He was similar to a ghost, appearing in the natural world but still existing only in the spiritual world. They simply could not accept the idea that God could have taken on flesh and come into this natural world.

The result of combining the Christian message with the ancient Greek worldview impacted tens of thousands of people. Adherents became known as "Gnostics." The word *gnostic* is derived from the Greek word *gnosis,* which means "knowledge," referring to how followers thought it required secret knowledge to understand God and the things of the spiritual world. Gnosticism became a huge issue within Christianity during the first two centuries when Christianity was spreading to the Greek-minded population.

Knowing this gives us more understanding of John's writings. Not only did he start off his Gospel declaring that the Word was God, but he went on to write:

And the Word became flesh, and dwelt among us…(John 1:14).

32

John declared that God became flesh. This truth directly challenged the early cult of Gnosticism.

In his first letter, John started off with similar words:

What was from the beginning, what we have heard, what we have seen with our eyes, what we have looked at and touched with our hands, concerning the Word of Life... (1 John 1:1).

Do you see how clearly John is fighting the cult of Gnosticism? He was telling his readers that he and the other apostles saw Jesus, they heard Him, and they touched Him. Jesus was God and He actually was manifested in the natural realm.

This truth, that God came into the natural realm, was easier to grasp for a person with the ancient Hebrew worldview. Because they envisioned no wall between the natural and spiritual realms, it was not difficult for them to conceive of the possibility of God manifesting in flesh.

God Manifested Himself in the Natural Realm in Jesus

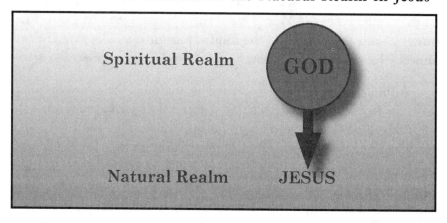

For the ancient Greek people, the wall that separated, in their minds, the spiritual world from the natural world made it difficult to conceive of a God who would come into the natural world.

Compare this with the thought patterns of the primitive tribe we discussed earlier, which separated everything into sharp objects and soft objects. They had a difficult time seeing animals as similar to one another because they put some animals in the sharp category and others in the soft category. The foundation of their thought patterns limited their ability to grasp certain realities. The Gnostics of the first and second centuries were similarly limited.

The early Church vigorously combated Gnostic teachings and gradually reduced their influence. After diminishing the Gnostic influence, the early Church faced the long and arduous struggle to define both the divinity and humanity of Jesus. The council of Nicaea in A.D. 325 stated the Church's position on this and related issues. Although many topics were addressed, one of the greatest triumphs was the result of seeing the nature of Jesus as it can only be seen apart from the ancient Greek spiritual/natural division. That triumph put the historical Church firmly on a path of truth.

Of course, some Gnostic writings still remain today, occasionally resurrected by various sects (such as the proponents of the book and movie entitled *The Da Vinci Code*). There are also various groups that struggle with the concept of the Trinity, but for the most part, the historical Church settled the related issues by the fifth century.

Although the Church succeeded in defining the nature of Jesus apart from the ancient Greek spiritual/natural division, the fundamental thought pattern of separating the spiritual world from the natural world continues to lie at the foundation of Western thought. The resulting influence has molded the minds of the Western world and remains the lens through which we view the world.

Discussion Questions

1. How might God be viewed through the Western worldview versus the Hebrew worldview?

2. How might we expect God to relate to us based on our view of Him?

Chapter 4

SECOND MAJOR OUTWORKING: ASCETICISM

THE ANCIENT GREEK WORLD profoundly influenced early Christianity because it was the dominant culture among the groups surrounding Israel, and because many Christian thinkers eagerly embraced it. Great teachers such as Justin, Origen, Clement, and Augustine believed that all truth is God's truth. Therefore, they concluded that the teachings of pagans like Socrates, Plato, and Aristotle should be included in their own teachings. They believed that by knowing what the Greek philosophers knew, as well as what Christians knew, they would then know more than the pagans.

It is true that in some ways knowledge was increased because of this mixture of Greek and Christian thought. However, in this book we are questioning that foundation and seeing how the ancient Greek worldview distorted Christian thought.

One example worth noting is from the life of Origen. As we mentioned earlier, Greek-minded people thought of the natural world as insignificant; and by the end of the first century many saw the world as corrupt. Seeing the natural world this way, Origen lived much of his life denying himself natural pleasures (sleeping on the floor and walking barefoot, for example). His negative view toward sex is evidenced by the fact that he made himself a eunuch by crushing his own testicles with two bricks.

Similar rejection of the natural world can be seen in the lives of numerous devout Christians who withdrew from society and embraced ascetic lifestyles. The most famous of these hermits was a leader named Anthony (A.D. 251-356). He lived in the Egyptian desert and set a high standard for holiness. Leaders like Anthony noted that Jesus lived a simple life, did not marry, and had no place to lay His head. In their efforts to emulate our Lord, thousands of Christians withdrew from society and lived in caves, isolated shacks, or monastic communities. During the third and fourth centuries, these communities spread out from Egypt into Greece, Palestine, Syria, and then farther east.

Although some great teachings and other benefits came out of the early monastic movement, a student of history cannot but wonder how much those hermits and monks were influenced by the Greek worldview. Seeing the world as corrupt, it was only reasonable—consciously or subconsciously—to conclude that withdrawal from the affairs of the world was the path to true holiness and godliness.

Strict asceticism led to an aberrant form of Christianity, but it would be wrong to label all of those devout Christians as deceived. Many of them had the proper view that physical pleasures can simply be distractions from their pursuit of God. Hence, their devotion and undistracted affection opened the door for true intimacy with God. However, there were others who misunderstood what God desired from them, and they withdrew from society based on the philosophical idea that the natural world is evil.

To see how different the monastic worldview was from the ancient Hebrew worldview, consider their divergent understandings of God's blessings. The Hebrew people had a very clear understanding that if God blessed them then those blessings would be evident in the natural, physical realm. In fact, the foundation of Hebrew law and thought was that God would bless those who obeyed Him, and those blessings would be tangible things such as the abundance of possessions, good health, prolific offspring, victory over enemies, a good reputation, lending rather than borrowing, and leading rather than following. These promised blessings were clearly stated in Deuteronomy 28:1-14. In the same chapter of Deuteronomy, God warned the Hebrew people that they would be cursed if they did not obey Him. He outlined some of those curses, including poverty, sickness, confusion, defeat, famine, drought, fear, wayward children, family discord, marital turmoil, slavery, and bondage (see Deut. 28:15-68). For the Hebrews, the blessings of God were not merely mystical feelings of well-being but real possessions and dominion in the natural realm.

Most of the hermits of the third and fourth centuries had no such association between the spiritual world and the natural world. They considered themselves blessed, and they even believed God would increase His blessings upon them, as they completely abandoned the natural pleasures of life.

It is worth repeating that some great teachings and lessons did come out of the early monastic movement. However, we cannot help but notice how it developed as Christianity was merging with the Greek worldview. The resulting thought patterns not only sent the hermits into isolation, but they have continued to influence the Church throughout her existence.

That influence can be seen in the values embraced by the Church during the fourth and fifth centuries as she was coming under the dominating influence of religious leaders in Rome. Celibacy was encouraged among the clergy, and, eventually (A.D. 1074), it became Canon Law under Pope Gregory VII. During the Middle Ages many of the cardinals and bishops lived opulent lives, but the majority of men and women in religious orders took vows of poverty. This was still seen as a step toward holiness.

Asceticism gradually decreased as Christianity moved into the Middle Ages. Monasteries played a major role in setting a new standard, especially as a result of Saint Benedict, who in the sixth century wrote the Benedictine rule, insisting that brothers live by the labor of their own hands. In 1323, Pope John XXII condemned as heretical the Franciscan claim that all things should be common property and that only by embracing poverty could the individual truly imitate Christ. With these positions taken by Church leaders, the ascetic idea that piety is associated with rejection of the world faded.

Although asceticism diminished, even today there are some ascetic values lingering among certain groups, and in particular, certain religious sects. Some Christians may not be aware of their own ascetic tendencies but they still (consciously or subconsciously) feel guilty when they experience great natural blessings. They focus on Scriptures that seem to elevate the value of poverty (e.g., Jesus telling the rich man to sell everything in Matthew 19:21; and the parable of the rich man and Lazarus in Luke 16:19-25), rather than those Scriptures that portray prosperity as a blessing from God (e.g., God's blessings upon Abraham, Joseph, and Solomon). Those Christians continue to think that it is more holy to be poor than to be wealthy. They also have deep underlying feelings that life should be hard and that they are only doing God's will if it is difficult.

In suggesting that asceticism may lead to an aberrant form of Christianity, I do not mean to imply that people less fortunate than ourselves are out of God's will. We live in a real world with real trials. Circumstances in developing nations can be difficult. Some people are called by God to endure more than others. It would be wrong to point our fingers at those less fortunate and conclude that they are less blessed than ourselves. God does, indeed, work in each person's life as He chooses.

What I do hope you can embrace is the idea that God's spiritual blessings result in physical blessings. There is no wall between the spiritual and natural realms.

Discussion Questions

1. What parallels can you draw from the modern Church regarding the value the historical Church placed on asceticism?

2. How can Christians strike a balance between the love of natural things and the avoidance of materialism?

3. When God says He will bless us, where should we expect His blessings to be manifested? In the spiritual world, or in the natural world?

4. How are we to live out the biblical injunction to be "in this world, but not of it"?

Chapter 5

Augustine's Ideas Seated in the Western Mind

W̶E CANNOT EXAMINE the development of the Western world-view without discussing the key role played by Augustine (A.D. 354-430). Augustine was a prominent theologian living at a critical time when thousands of people throughout the Roman Empire were flooding into the Church. Being a student of Greek thought, he was able to communicate the Christian message in terms that the educated elite and the common masses could easily comprehend.

Before converting to Christianity, Augustine was trained in Neo-Platonism, the philosophy of a third-century teacher named Plotinus. His philosophy was called Neo-Platonism because it was a reworking of Plato's ideas based on the concept of the spiritual realm being the real world and the natural world being insignificant. Plotinus also saw God as a huge, glowing force filling the spiritual world. This concept was deeply seated in the brilliant young mind of Augustine.

With this foundation, Augustine began investigating Christianity. Seeing God as an all-powerful force radiating truth and light, he concluded that God was in control of all things. Augustine was well-known for his concept of an all-controlling God, so I am not going to take time to develop how he came to this conclusion. (If you are interested in learning more, I refer you to another book I have written entitled *Who Is God?*, which explains Augustine's understanding on these and related ideas.) The key point is that Augustine's concept of God as being an all-powerful, all-controlling force became inserted in the foundation of Western Christianity.

Augustine not only was a Neo-Platonist, but as a young Christian he spent much time in a sect called Manichaeism. This sect clearly separated the spiritual world from the natural world and also identified the natural world as corrupt and evil. Later on, Augustine parted from the sect of Manichaeism and tried to distinguish his teachings by pointing out some of the errors of Manichaeism. However, he continued to hold a strong division between the spiritual and natural worlds, along with a negative view of the natural world.

As a consequence, Augustine developed his theology laying biblical truths upon the foundation of the spiritual/natural division. For Augustine, the natural world was temporary and corrupt. However, he saw an all-powerful, all-consuming God controlling all things in both the spiritual and natural worlds.

Augustine's View After Becoming a Christian

GOD

Natural World: Insignificant and Corrupt

Augustine's negative view of this natural world can be seen in his understanding of sexual desires and original sin. He saw physical desires as that which tie humanity to this corrupt, natural world, and sexual passions as the strongest, most corrupt desires. This belief was especially significant in his own mind because he lived a sexually promiscuous lifestyle before becoming Christian, and he continued wrestling with sexual temptations for almost all of his life.[1] With a very negative view of sexual desires, Augustine believed that the sin of Adam is passed to all of humanity as men and women express sexual passions toward one another.

He also believed that Adam's sin released a moral corruption so devastating that humans are born with no ability to resist sin. In Augustine's mind, babies are born radically selfish, that is, totally subject to human passions and desires. He equated that selfishness with sinfulness.

These beliefs came to the forefront of Christian thought as Augustine engaged in intellectual battles with a British monk named Pelagius. Taking the opposing view, Pelagius taught that infants are born innocent and as they grow they develop the ability to choose good or evil. He argued that people are created in God's image and are morally free. Augustine would have also said that people are created in God's image, but in his mind that concept took second place to the more obvious fact that people are sinners.

Augustine's and Pelagius' views became so divisive that supporters of both views rioted in the streets of Rome in A.D. 417. Two years later, two councils of bishops in Palestine declared Pelagius' views as orthodox. However, two opposing councils of African bishops, under the direction of Augustine, condemned Pelagius. Soon afterward Pope Innocent sided with the African leaders. When he died, his successor, Pope Zosimus, first declared Pelagius' teachings orthodox, but later reversed his decision and excommunicated Pelagius. The battle continued for more than ten years, with Pelagius' devout follower, Julian of Eclanum, taking over after the death of Pelagius.[2]

Although Augustine ultimately won the battle in the eyes of the Church, the Roman Catholic Church did not fully embrace Augustine's teachings. Pope Gregory softened Augustine's negative view by saying that people inherit Adam's sin, but not his guilt. Thomas Aquinas taught that our will is bent by sin but not determined completely toward evil. There has been much discussion and disagreement throughout Church history concerning the nature of humanity, but Augustine's negative view has held the dominant position and came to the forefront again through Martin Luther and John Calvin (both of whom we will discuss later).[3]

When he wrote about the world, Augustine spoke of the beauty and grandeur of God's creation, yet he saw that the sin of Adam released a devastating moral corruption upon all of creation. He contemplated the curse released in the Garden of Eden, noting that thorns now grow on plants, men have to work by the sweat of their brow, and pain has increased as women give birth to children. According to Augustine, the sin of Adam released upon the whole natural world a sentence of death, thus making this natural world a harsh, cruel, and miserable place to live.

Augustine's understanding that this world is insignificant and temporary can be seen in his book entitled *The City of God.* His writing of this book was stirred by the conquest of Rome in 410 A.D. Christians before that date had great hopes that God would raise up the city of Rome to be the center of Christendom. They thought of it as God's city; but when it was destroyed, their hopes were dashed. Augustine addressed these issues by explaining in his book how the true city of God is not on earth but up in Heaven. A clear distinction of a glorious city in Heaven versus a temporal, insignificant city on earth fit well with Augustine's worldview based in Greek thought.

Augustine wrestled through many other issues of the time. For example, he played key roles in settling the issues concerning the nature of Jesus, capitalism, and freedom for all people. So extensive was his work that thousands of books have been written about him and his thoughts and beliefs. However, we will be focusing on the three foundational points that Augustine most profoundly contributed to the Western worldview:

1. God is in control.

2. Humanity is inherently evil.

3. This world is corrupt.

Historians and theologians generally agree that Augustine's theology has dominated Christian thought since the fifth century.

Augustine's Thoughts Inserted Into Western Thought

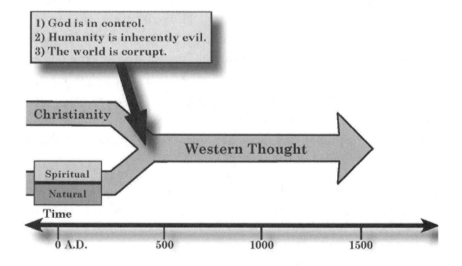

There are innumerable implications of Augustine's theology, but I will mention just a few of the most obvious implications of the three points listed above.

People who have embraced Augustine's first point can reassure themselves that God is in control no matter how difficult the circumstances are around them. That can be comforting, but on the negative side it leads to fatalistic, victimization tendencies. If people experience poverty or disease, they reason that it has been ordained by God. They also tend to accept without question their allotted roles within society.

Augustine's second point that all of humanity is inherently evil led to the greater empowerment of the established Church and government. As people became convinced that they are helplessly under the control of sin, they saw the need for outside intervention. They reasoned that good is outside of man and not within man, so the Church and government were necessary to control evil. Hence, Augustine is seen as one of the major influencers who empowered the Roman Catholic Church and European governments during the Middle Ages.

Augustine's third point—that this world is corrupt—determined his view of eternity. He concluded that Heaven must be the state in which Christians will escape their bodies and lives in this miserable natural world. As a result, the historical Church developed a concept of Heaven where God's people will experience a bodiless eternity, floating around on the clouds singing praises to God forever. In reality, the Bible gives us a picture of our eternal existence that includes new glorified bodies living in a new Heaven and a new earth (see 1 Cor. 15:42-44; Rev. 21).

Augustine impacted Christianity in many other ways—some positive and some negative—but in the coming pages we will only make further reference to his three foundational ideas concerning God, humanity, and the world.

	Augustinian Thought
I. God	In Control
II. Humanity	Inherently Evil
III. World	Corrupt

Today, people may question the validity of these three points, but they are still profoundly influenced by the related thought patterns. These points are so deeply rooted in our history and culture that everyone in Western society, to some degree, has their thoughts molded to fit into the related categories. This will become more evident as we continue following the development of Western thought through history.

Discussion Questions

1. What do you think about Augustine's main tenets?

    a. Is God in control? To what extent?

    b. Is mankind inherently evil?

    c. Is the world corrupt? To what extent?

2. If you had lived in Augustine's times, would you have sided with his views, or those of Pelagius? Why?

3. Would you have been passionate enough about your view to join the riots in the streets of Rome?

Chapter 6

THE MIDDLE AGES AND THE DARK AGES

HISTORIANS CONSIDER the Middle Ages to be the period from the fall of the Roman Empire in A.D. 476 to the beginning of the Protestant Reformation in the early 16th century.

The Middle Ages

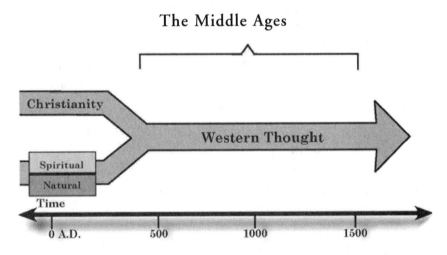

The Middle Ages experienced what can be said of many time periods: "It was the best of times and it was the worst of times." On the negative side, people seemed helpless under the overbearing influence of spiritual powers. They were ever conscious of the overwhelming control that things in the spiritual world—God, angels, demons, and other spiritual forces—had over their lives and the natural world. Superstition was rampant. Sickness was considered either an act of God or the result of demonic activity. Life was hard and people expected it to be so. Hope for the righteous rested in the pleasures awaiting them in the afterlife. The possibility of being thrown into hell was real, and writings such as *Dante's Inferno,* kept hell on the forefront of people's minds.

Within the Middle Ages was the period sometimes referred to as the "Dark Ages" (circa A.D. 400-1000). Europeans of the time did not see themselves in any type of Dark Ages, but scholars in the 18th and 19th centuries looked back on that period very critically. Thinking of themselves as advanced and the product of the Scientific Revolution, they labeled the period out of which society had emerged as the Dark Ages. (They labeled their own period as the "Enlightenment," which we will examine later.)

The Dark Ages were difficult but not as dark, primitive, or unscientific as many modern people think.[1] It was during this period that Europe became Christianized. Of course, this is the very thing of which some modern non-Christian historians are critical. Indeed, the established Church exercised great authority over the common people. However, we need to also consider the positive spiritual and moral advancements made throughout Europe. It was the expansion of the Church, more than any other factor, that displaced pagan views and established civilization. Christian values permeated society and became enforced by civil law.

Great advancements were also made in areas such as technology, commerce, and science. Historian Rodney Stark, in his excellent book entitled *The Victory of Reason,* explains how European technology and science of the period overtook the rest of the world. Water mills were developed and built across Europe, which enabled people to efficiently cut lumber and stones, turn lathes, grind knives and swords, hammer metal, and make pulp to produce paper. Wind mills were also employed to pump water for irrigation and the drainage of large wetlands. Cloth making was mechanized, and more versatile plows opened up huge areas for farming. Tremendous changes also happened throughout society as a result of the invention of eyeglasses, chimneys, and clocks. The development of round ships and compasses opened up the world to travel by water. Land transportation was revolutionized by the invention of horse collars and wagons with brakes and front axles that could swivel.[2]

A historically accurate view of the Middle Ages recognizes that the vast majority of people lived much better at that time than they did in the ancient Greek and Roman periods. Hundreds of examples could be given to show this, but let's simply consider the invention of the chimney. Before homes had chimneys, people lived in unheated shelters or in homes filled with smoke. Without chimneys, people smelled like smoke, breathed toxic air, and often ate uncooked food. With chimneys as only one of many advancements, we can be assured that life for the common people in the Middle Ages was better than it was for them during the Greek and Roman Empires.

Of course, by our modern standards they still lived difficult lives. They lived as victims to the forces of nature such as storms and diseases. Transitioning out of a victim mentality was a slow process taking several hundred years. One of the most important turning points resulted from the writings of Thomas Aquinas (A.D. 1225-1274), who taught that man's will is fallen but not his intellect. This led to the understanding that man's intellect can arrive at truth, which opened the door for intellectual endeavors of all sorts, including the Scientific Revolution of the 16th and 17th centuries.

Toward the last half of the Middle Ages, more than 80 universities were founded in Europe, almost all of them dedicated primarily to producing clergy for the Church. Theology and philosophy were king and queen in the kingdom of education. All students were expected to master these subjects. It was during this period that the writings of the ancient Greek philosophers reentered into the mainstream of European intellectual thought.

I cannot overemphasize how the universities and intellectual endeavors of the later Middle Ages more deeply established a mental division between the spiritual and natural worlds. With Aristotle's writings being given prominence, his fundamental thought patterns were applied to every area of life. The intellectual European world already had Greek thought at the foundation of their thought patterns, but then intense application of philosophical thought carved these patterns more deeply into their minds. With theology and philosophy as king and queen, biblical truths were interpreted in the context of the spiritual/natural division.

The Spiritual/Natural Division Was Reinforced in the Latter Part of the Middle Ages Among the Educated

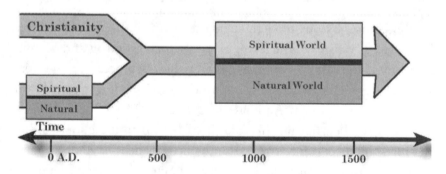

Considering the history we have just studied, you may wonder: *Is it even possible for a modern Western person to think without the spiritual/natural division?* Well, it *is* very difficult. Categories are necessary for any person to organize his or her thoughts. Every person has a mind filled with categories. What we can do is attempt to analyze our own thought patterns and perhaps identify some of the ways these have limited our thinking, narrowed our view, and caused us to drift into error. That is what this study attempts to do as we advance through history.

Discussion Questions

1. What impact does fear of the supernatural have on the advancement of humanity?

2. What role does fear of the supernatural play in the ability to control people?

3. How did universities of the Middle Ages differ from modern universities today?

4. In what ways did the teachings of Thomas Aquinas lay the foundation for the Scientific Revolution?

Chapter 7

THE RENAISSANCE AND PROTESTANT REFORMATION

T OWARD THE END OF THE MIDDLE AGES, the stage was being prepared for a major shift in thinking. The Hundred Years War (1337-1453) between England and France ended. The Black Death (1348-1354), which had killed nearly one third of Europe, passed. Literacy was on the rise. A fresh beginning was being offered to the European nations. The stage was set for the emerging Renaissance.

The word *renaissance* is a French word meaning "rebirth," which is derived from Latin *renasci, re+nasci,* to be reborn. During this period, scholars and artists wanted the spirit of human achievement, which was so evident in classical, pre-Christian antiquity, to be reborn. Hence, their studies focused on the learning and art of ancient Greece and Rome. This emphasis began in Italy in the 1300s, then gradually spread across all of Europe.

This period was accompanied by significant human achievements. The Portuguese reopened the trade route to China by sailing around the southern tip of Africa. Columbus landed in the New World. The Gutenberg printing press was invented. Books like Thomas More's *Utopia* inspired readers to dream of a bright future. Artists like Leonardo da Vinci and Michelangelo captured the spirit of the age in proclaiming the potential and grandeur of humanity.

During the Renaissance, people questioned authority. The time was ripe for challenging religious authorities, and strong leaders began speaking against the corruption in the priesthood. Scandals among the clergy were becoming publicly known. Martin Luther could be quiet no longer once he saw indulgences (in Roman Catholic thought, these are the allowances given to people to free them from the punishment of their sins) being sold to raise money for the construction of St. Peter's Basilica. His 95 theses were nailed to a church door in Wittenberg, Germany (1517). The Protestant Reformation erupted and within 50 years one half of Europe left Roman Catholicism.

The Renaissance and Protestant Reformation

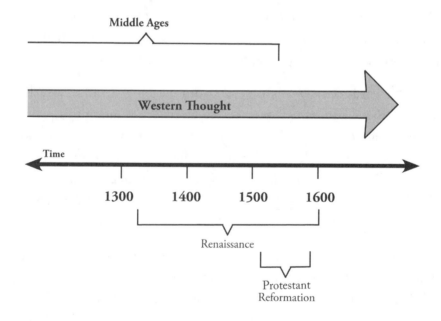

Countless volumes have been written about that period, but we are especially interested in the spiritual/natural separation that lies at the foundation of Western thought. During the Reformation, a few chinks were made in that wall of division. Martin Luther boldly declared that marriage was a holy arrangement, and he himself took a wife. This not only challenged Roman Catholic tradition, but also shook the underlying beliefs that holiness required celibacy and holy people kept themselves from the affairs of this world.

	Augustinian, Lutheran, and Calvinistic Thought
I. God	In Control
II. Humanity	Inherently Evil
III. World	Corrupt

John Calvin pushed truth even further by declaring that all vocations are holy, and therefore, people called to work with their hands are just as called by God as persons called to the priesthood.

Even though Luther and Calvin each pointed out an area in which the spiritual/natural division should not apply, they still maintained the spiritual/natural division as the foundation of their thinking.[1] Both Luther and Calvin also clung tightly to their Augustinian roots, each holding to the three points of Augustinian thought that we identified earlier.

These fundamental ideas continued to dominate European thought until the Scientific Revolution, which we will discuss in the next chapter.

Discussion Questions

1. Is the challenging of authority a necessary component of a revolution?

2. To what extent was Christianity responsible for the Dark Ages?

3. To what extent was Christianity responsible for the Renaissance?

Chapter 8

Birth of the Modern World Through Science

THE RENAISSANCE was followed by the Scientific Revolution of the 16th and 17th centuries. That revolution brought the world into what we know as the Modern Period.

The Scientific Revolution

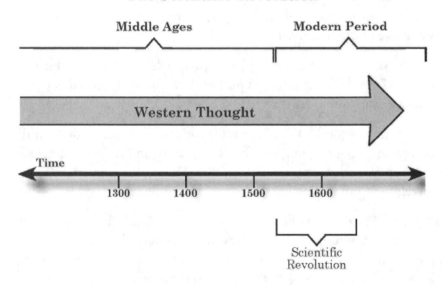

There were many notable events that led up to the Scientific Revolution. One of the most important transitions took place as Augustine (profoundly influenced by Plato) was overshadowed by Thomas Aquinas (who relied heavily upon Aristotle). Augustine's teachings had led the common people to accept what their leaders told them, and the intellectual leadership developed much of their understanding of truth by reasoning about intangible ideas. In contrast, Aristotle had taught that truth is developed as people focus on real things that can be seen and touched in this physical world. This refocus occurred as Aristotle's writing came to the forefront in the late Middle Ages, and then leaders like Thomas Aquinas concluded that truth can be derived from observing this natural world.

These and many other events led up to the Scientific Revolution, but historians often mark its actual start at the publication in 1543 of Nicolaus Copernicus' book, *On the Revolution of the Celestial Spheres.*[1] Copernicus' work in this book showed that the sun was the center of our solar system rather than the earth.

Galileo Galilei (1564-1642) took the revolution another step by studying astronomy and declaring that the entire universe is understandable in mathematical terms.

Next came Francis Bacon (1561-1626) who insisted that the world may be known through human observation, and that, indeed, an entire universe waited to be discovered.

Isaac Newton (1647-1727) walked through the open door of discovery and, by observing the forces of gravity and motion, concluded that all of nature functioned with regularity and consistency—and therefore, it can be known.

Each of these "fathers of the Scientific Revolution" were theists (believers in God). However, their revolutionary thinking challenged the worldview of their time. Previously, most people thought of God as being in direct control of all things. After the Scientific Revolution, God was seen as the One who started the universe but then let the universe function according to the natural, predictable laws that He set up at

Creation—as if God were the great "clock maker" who created the clock, wound it up, and then let it go (a view called Deism).

Once this worldview was embraced by influential thinkers, they were free to apply their reasoning abilities to understanding the physical world. No longer were their studies in astronomy undermined by thoughts that stars may be moved about by angelic beings. As soon as they concluded that the human body functions according to predictable laws and that diseases are not the result of demonic activity, then studies in medicine flourished. This revolutionary thinking launched scientific discovery, which, in turn, advanced almost every area of life.

Worldview of the Scientific Revolution: The World Functions According to Natural Laws That God Set Up at Creation

From that time forward, the path to discovery became known as the *Scientific Method,* which is the idea that knowledge can only be obtained through observation and testing.

We should be grateful for the innumerable advancements that the science of the modern period has given to humanity, but notice that the ancient Greek philosophers' separation between the spiritual and the natural worlds still lies at the foundation of Western thought. Now, however, the spiritual world decreased in significance as the natural world emerged on the scene—almost as if it alone exists.

The Fundamental Change in Thought Patterns Emerging From the Scientific Revolution

Spiritual World: Insignificant

**The Real World
Natural World: World of Reason
World of Science**

This worldview became ever more dominant in the 17th and 18th centuries. It became largely fixed in the minds of the Western world after Charles Darwin published his *Origin of Species* in 1859 and *The Descent of Man* in 1871. Once humanity's existence was explained without God's involvement, God was pushed farther out of the consciousness of those He created.

Discussion Questions

1. How did it come to be that humanity's greatest period of scientific advancement was also a period during which God was pushed farther away from the consciousness of people?

2. What are some of the positive and negative aspects of removing the supernatural dimension when studying this natural world?

Chapter 9

THE GREAT WALL
DIVIDING FAITH FROM REASON

WITH THE SCIENTIFIC REVOLUTION came another transition in thought pertaining to how faith was categorized within the world of the spirit. It was not that the early scientists rejected faith or the spiritual world. They simply concluded that things in the natural world could be observed and tested, while things in the spiritual world were not subject to these human activities. As a consequence, faith was thought to be the antithesis of reason—and less respectable intellectually.

Transition in the Understanding of Faith

Spiritual World: Realm of Faith

Natural World: World of Reason

This separation was not the sole work of scientists. It was developed over the course of many years in both the Church and the secular world. The clear demarcation between faith and reason was a natural outworking—almost the inevitable outworking—of the fundamental ancient Greek worldview. In fact, about 300 B.C., the Greek philosopher Epicurus, along with his followers, came to a worldview much like that brought forth in the Scientific Revolution.[1] The separation between faith and reason became more clearly defined as the Scientific Revolution swept across Europe. Soon scientists and philosophers were using this separation of faith from reason as the foundation of their discussions and thought.

Years later, philosopher-pastor Soren Kierkegaard (1813-1855) pitted faith against reason when he argued that religious faith is irrational since it always involves accepting that which is absurd. Kierkegaard's book, *Fear and Trembling,* discusses Abraham offering his son to God. In this he argued that God requires us to hold beliefs that are ridiculous. Still desiring to encourage people in spiritual things, Kierkegaard spoke of "taking a leap of faith." When he and others spoke of taking a "blind leap," they were tacitly agreeing that having faith means accepting as fact something for which one has no proof.

If we admit that there is no proof for beliefs, then we are admitting that we really cannot be sure if they are true. In other words, whatever cannot be observed is *unknowable.* Hence, the separation between faith and reason also became understood as the separation between the unknowable and the knowable. This dichotomy lies at the foundation of modern Western thought.

Since the 18th century, God and religion have also been assigned to the world of the spirit. This is especially prevalent in our institutions of higher learning and so I will refer to this form of the Western worldview as Western intellectualism.

The Worldview of Modern Western Intellectualism

Unknowable
Spiritual World: Realm of Faith, GOD, and Religion

Knowable
Natural World: Reason and Science

Many prominent scientists today have seized onto this dichotomy and promoted it as the only reasonable way to view the world. For example, the famous biologist Stephen Gould so compartmentalized the spiritual from the natural that he taught that science and faith should occupy separate "non-overlapping magisteria."[2] Famous evolutionist Richard Dawkins said:

> Faith is the great cop-out, the great excuse to evade the need to think and evaluate evidence. Faith is belief in spite of, even perhaps because of, a lack of evidence....Faith, being belief that isn't based on evidence, is the principle vice of any religion."[3]

Leaders like these, who have been heralded as the heroes of modern scientific thought, have not only separated the spiritual from the natural world, but succeeded in creating a huge chasm between the two. Some atheistic scientists go so far as to totally eliminate the spiritual realm from their worldview. For example, the astronomer, Carl Sagan, is famous for his saying, "The cosmos is all there is or ever was or ever will be."

The Worldview of Modern
Western Intellectualism

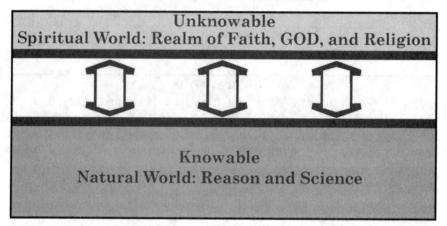

Of course, not all modern scientists embrace this worldview. In 1916 a survey was taken of biologists, physicists, and mathematicians in which they were asked if they believe in a God who actively communicates with people and to whom one may pray and expect an answer. The same survey was taken in 1997. Both times about 40 percent answered in the affirmative.[4]

Unfortunately, it is the atheistic thinkers who often get in the limelight and capture world headlines. Furthermore, their way of thinking does influence all of us. Their underlying worldview is not always evident to the average person reading their books or listening to their lectures, but as their atheistic worldview is applied to all areas of study, students consciously and subconsciously place facts into the two categories of their dichotomous worldview. Soon the students are looking at life, nature, society, business, art, people, government, history, and the future through the worldview of modern Western intellectualism.

This worldview is subtly imposed upon the Western mind and remains the vocal rallying point of atheists today. One of the most popular atheistic books of our time reveals this when the author boldly states, "…every religion preaches the truth of propositions for which no evidence is even conceivable."[5]

A major outworking of this way of thinking is that all forms of religion are thought to be unprovable and unknowable with no way to distinguish the validity of one over the other. Even if a person values religion, it is considered a blind leap, and as such, it is unimportant as to which leap is taken. One person's religion works for them while a second person's different religion works for them. Absolute truth is not sought nor expected, since no religion can be tested or verified. A person who has embraced the worldview of Western intellectualism will conclude that all religions are equally valid (or invalid). Someone who values his own religion as more valid than others is thought to be judgmental, uneducated, and intolerant.

The individual indoctrinated into this worldview tends to avoid serious discussions about God and religion. Since no religion can be verified, what is the use? Since reason does not apply to the spiritual world, there is no sense in attempting to use reason. The person who continues to believe in God, but is indoctrinated in Western intellectualism, is comfortable leaving God distant and unknowable—or mysterious. They may speak of God in a sterile fashion, but the idea that a human being may know God is beyond their grasp.

Also, values and ethics become relative within Western intellectualism. If God and religion are unprovable and, therefore, unknowable, then right and wrong are unprovable and unknowable. All such things are matters of blind acceptance rather than reason, according to Western intellectualism.

What is tragic is that Western Christians are profoundly influenced by these thought patterns. There is a saying often used in debates of logic that goes like this, "whoever frames the argument wins the argument." By framing discussions concerning faith, God, religion, and ethics within the spiritual/natural division, people who are antagonistic toward Christianity are predetermining many of the conclusions. Christians who allow themselves to be trapped in the spiritual/natural division are giving up the debate before the debate begins. They are abandoning the worldview upon which Christianity was originally laid before it was relaid on the foundation of Greek thought.

The Worldview of Modern Western Intellectualism

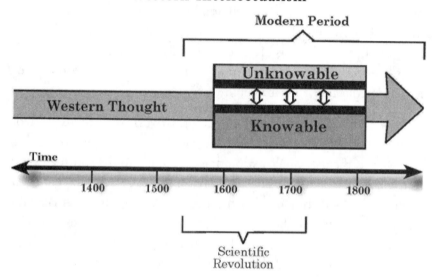

In the next four chapters we will see that this worldview of Western intellectualism is unfounded and indefensible.

Discussion Questions

1. When scientists like Richard Dawkins say, "Faith is the great cop-out, the great excuse to evade the need to think and evaluate evidence," what do you think he means by "faith"?

2. How is it that certain scientists and other intellectual leaders can deny God and yet bring blessings to God's people?

Chapter 10

INTEGRATION OF THE
SPIRITUAL AND NATURAL REALMS

IN THE INTRODUCTION of this book, I said that I would develop a Christian worldview in Section II, but I cannot wait that long to correct a major error that is now obvious in the development of the Western worldview. The fathers of the Scientific Revolution launched science into many wonderful advancements, but when they pitted faith against reason they opened the door for an avalanche of confusion and errors. To stop that avalanche in our minds, let's sink an anchor into truth. To do this we must go all the way back to the foundation of the ancient Hebrew worldview, which sees the spiritual and natural realms as fully integrated one into the other.

In this chapter we will briefly examine the three key areas of science, religion, and faith. Contrary to what modern Western intellectualism says, we will see that these three areas incorporate both the spiritual and natural realms.

First, consider how scientific thought was first developed during the Scientific Revolution. The endeavors of the early scientists were not even called "science" during that period of history. Their studies were known as "natural philosophy." They started with the philosophical idea that God is a rational Being, and therefore, the universe He created must function according to rationally understandable laws.

The early scientists were only able to conclude that the universe functions according to rational laws because they were monotheists (they believed there was one God). Polytheists—who envision many divine beings involved in this world—form an understanding of a universe that is unstable, being tossed to and fro as those gods interact and pursue their individual interests. Polytheists have no basis on which to conclude that the universe functions according to rationally understandable laws. This is the reason that science has only flourished historically in the monotheistic cultures of Christianity, Islam, and Judaism.[1]

Monotheism Gave Birth to Science

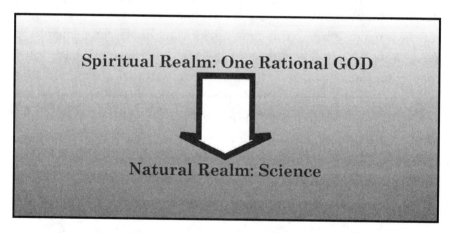

Spiritual Realm: One Rational GOD

Natural Realm: Science

The understanding that there is one rational God was the starting point of modern science, and even today, science and faith in God are fully integrated for those willing to admit it. Allan Rex Sandage, one of the most respected and known scientists in the world, converted from atheism to theism as a result of his scientific studies. As he pointed out, "Many scientists are now driven to faith by their very work."[2] The noted scientist and philosopher Stephen C. Myers said,

"...the testimony of science supports theism....Science, done right, points toward God."[3]

Science Points Toward God

Next, let's consider religion to see how wrong it is to categorize it within the spiritual realm. Modern Western intellectualism portrays religion as a mystical belief in some untouchable Being, which has little to no effect upon what people do in the natural world. As a result, people with this worldview tend to think it is wrong to take into account a person's religious beliefs when making decisions such as who to hire for a position or to elect for a political office.

In contrast, people who have a more traditional Western worldview take someone's religion very seriously. They understand that religion influences what people do in their political, social, and private life. It influences how individuals treat their spouse, children, and neighbor. Religion is evident every day in the natural realm as we watch people react to the daily trials and successes of life. Religion is so much of a natural thing that we can examine the financial records of almost any human being and determine, from their spending habits, to which religion they adhere. Contrary to what modern Western intellectualism likes to portray, religion is spiritual *and* natural.

Religion Is Both
Spiritual and Natural

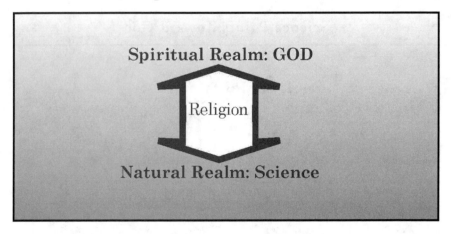

Finally, consider faith. The modern Western mind categorizes faith in the realm of the spirit and then asserts that faith is the blind acceptance of unproven religious ideas. Let's contrast this definition with the biblical use of the word *faith*.

Faith is a noun, and to understand what it means it is helpful to first define the corresponding verb *believe.* The apostle Paul explained:

...for with the heart a person believes... (Romans 10:10).

The heart being spoken of here is not the organ that pumps blood throughout the physical body. The heart in this context refers to the seat of faith, affections, and love. Believing is not a function of the intellect, but it is the action of putting one's faith, affections, and love in something and/or someone.

The heart of a person is always oriented toward something or someone. This means everyone believes in something and/or someone.

Believing Is the Orientation of One's Heart

People only place their heart in that which they have found to be worthy of love and faith—or in other words, what they have found to be trustworthy and true. Believing is never a blind leap. Believing is what people do with their heart, after they have done everything possible with their intellect to determine whether or not something is trustworthy. Furthermore, everyone is constantly observing and testing to see whether the object of their affections and belief is still trustworthy.

With this understanding of what it means to believe, we can now define faith. It is the bond resulting from belief. It is the anchor of a person's heart in something or someone. It is the connection established by belief.

Everyone has and uses faith. Some place their faith in themselves or other people. Others have their faith in government, business, science, or money. Some anchor their lives in spiritual things and others in natural things. All of us place our faith in different areas at different times.

When we speak of placing our faith in God, we are saying that we have concluded that He is real and worthy of our trust; and therefore, we have chosen to believe in Him. Faith in God is the connection established between a person and God. It is only established and maintained when a person has done much testing and reasoning to determine if God is worthy of one's trust. Contrary to what modern Western intellectualism says, faith in God is not limited to the spiritual realm, but is a connection between the natural and spiritual realms.

Biblical Understanding of Faith

In order to fully grasp the biblical view of faith, we must broaden our understanding even further. Faith in God is not only a general attachment to Him, but it may be an attachment to some specific benefit that God offers. The writer of Hebrews uses this definition when he tells us:

> *Now faith is the substance of things hoped for...*(Hebrews 11:1 KJV).

According to this verse, hope comes first and then faith follows. In this context, hope refers to a person desiring something from God with some level of expectancy. The writer of Hebrews goes on to explain how many great men and women hoped for something from God, but then one day their hope turned into faith. The point at which their hope turned into faith was when they *"obtained* [a] *witness"* (Heb. 11:4-5), or in other words, when they embraced within their heart a confidence or an assurance that God would provide what He had promised. Once the heart receives that assurance from God, things in the natural realm eventually change according to that which is believed. With this understanding we see that *faith is the connection by which a person brings things from the spiritual realm into the natural realm.*

This understanding of faith is beyond the grasp of people trained in Western intellectualism. The division between the spiritual and the natural is so deep and wide within their psyche that it is extremely difficult to make this transition in thought patterns. Compare this to the tribe who categorized everything into sharp objects and soft objects; they were unable to form in their mind a category for animals. Similarly, the modern Western intellectual has no category for religion or faith that incorporates both the spiritual and natural realms. Their definitions of religion and faith limit their understanding of these concepts to the spiritual realm.

Furthermore, Western intellectualism has no frame of reference for moving spiritual things into the natural realm. In other words, those who fully embrace the worldview of Western intellectualism have no place for miracles or for God to answer prayer. Yet, for miracles to happen all we need is a miracle-working God. It is reasonable for us to believe in the possibility of miracles if God exists and if He can intervene in this world. We will discover this God in the next two chapters.

Discussion Questions

1. Why is monotheism good for the scientific advancement of a society?

2. What do you see as the primary differences between hope and faith?

3. Can faith be unconscious? In other words, can we have faith and not realize it?

4. Why is faith considered a blind leap by some and a firm, rational decision by others?

Chapter 11

PROOF FOR THE EXISTENCE OF GOD

T HE WALL BETWEEN the spiritual and natural realms that has been imposed upon the Western mind is imaginary, groundless, and wrong. If people tear down that wall in their own mind, then proof of God's existence is available.

To see this, consider the declarative statement, "Stuff exists." At this point I am not defining what stuff is, but the fact that something exists is obvious.

Of course, a philosopher may respond by saying that everything may be an illusion in our own minds. A philosopher can stand at the foot of a huge mountain and through his skills at reasoning come to doubt the existence of the mountain upon which he stands and sees with his own eyes. For anyone but a philosopher, such a conclusion is foolishness and a child could justifiably say, "The emperor is naked." The child's wisdom is born out once the philosopher finishes his mental gymnastics then goes to eat a meal. No matter what the philosopher says, every philosopher believes that stuff exists and bases his life on this belief, evidenced by the fact that he eats stuff to keep himself alive.

The scientist more readily admits to the existence of stuff. In fact, everything she does lies on this foundation. No observation and testing can even begin until the scientist first establishes the fact for herself that stuff exists.

So then, let's start with the obvious: stuff exists.

Point number two: there had to have been a stuff creator.

The philosopher and atheist may object and claim that the stuff needed no creator, but to believe that stuff created itself or that the stuff always existed is worse than believing in magic. To believe that no one is responsible for all of this stuff is absurd.

This conclusion is obvious with the worldview of the Bible writers. The apostle Paul explained:

> *For since the creation of the world His invisible attributes, His eternal power and divine nature, have been clearly seen, being understood through what has been made, so that they are without excuse* (Romans 1:20).

This verse says more than what I am presently trying to show you, and I will discuss creation's evidence of God's attributes in the next chapter. Here it is enough to state that creation is declaring—shouting, announcing, giving undeniable proof—that there is (or at least *was*) a creator. The apostle Paul said that God's attributes are *"clearly seen."* Every human being is *"without excuse."*

Notice that Paul's worldview *did not assume the existence of God;* rather, his worldview *allowed him to see proof for the existence of God.* That is the most important sentence in this book, so allow me to restate it: Paul's worldview did not assume the existence of God; his worldview allowed him to see proof for the existence of God.

If you cannot see this, then you are still looking at the world through the groundless, indefensible, Western spiritual/natural division.

Your vision is distorted. Let down the imaginary wall within your own mind. If you are going to embrace Christianity separated from Western thought—and, in particular, the influence of Western philosophy—then you will immediately see that stuff exists, and therefore, there had to be a stuff creator.

The Worldview That Reveals Truth

> **Spiritual Realm**
>
>
>
> **Natural Realm**

Untold numbers of philosophers and theologians have argued to try to prove the existence of God. Most philosophers who lived and worked since the Scientific Revolution (followed by the Enlightenment, which we will examine shortly) have concluded that God's existence cannot be proven. But to people with no wall in their mind between the spiritual and natural realms, God's existence is obvious. As Paul wrote, every human being is already without excuse.

In case you are having difficulty seeing this, allow me to state it in a way that may help. I don't want to be facetious, but look around you—there is stuff. Hello! Is anyone home? Stuff exists; therefore, there had to be a stuff creator. There comes a time when people should quit arguing and just laugh at stupid ideas—and this includes the atheists' most cherished belief. I don't want to be rude; I want to make the obvious obvious. The acceptance of God's existence is not a blind leap. Just the opposite is true—to not believe in a stuff creator is to be blind to the obvious. It is absurd not to believe in a stuff creator.

Of course, we have lost the Western atheists in this discussion because the Scientific Revolution (and the Enlightenment that followed) set up in their minds a dichotomy of faith versus reason. Their definitions of faith and reason exclude God from the realm of reason. In reality, those categories are pure assumptions—false assumptions. Indeed, we cannot prove the existence of God to the atheist who refuses to let go of those assumed categories. In like fashion, we cannot prove the existence of bacteria to a person who refuses to look through a microscope and see the bacteria for himself. If, however, a person is willing to look through a microscope, then we can prove to him the existence of bacteria. Similarly, if an atheist is willing to look at the world, outside of his present dichotomous framework, then we can prove the existence of God.

Here it is: stuff exists, so a stuff creator exists (or at least existed in the past).

Atheistic readers may object and quickly argue that this is no argument for the existence of the Christian God. Indeed, I have not yet stated anything about this creator's nature, and to argue against the Christian God at this point is to change the subject. It is to dodge the bullet, to hide behind a smoke screen. So long as we define God as the stuff creator, it is absurd not to accept God's existence.

Discussion Questions

1. Why do atheists see belief in God as absurd?

2. What was it about Paul's worldview that allowed him to see proof for the existence of God?

Chapter 12

REASONABLE PEOPLE BELIEVE IN GOD

I N THE PRECEDING CHAPTER, we saw how the existence (if not in the present, then at least in the past) of a stuff creator is obvious and undeniable. An individual who has embraced the Western dichotomy of faith versus reason is blinded to this truth. Yet, it remains a truth.

Once we have established the existence of a stuff creator, we can go on to discover the creator's nature.

Look again at Paul's words:

For since the creation of the world His invisible attributes, His eternal power and divine nature, have been clearly seen, being understood through what has been made...(Romans 1:20).

Indeed, if we look at the stuff that exists, we can conclude some things about the stuff creator.

First, when we study the universe—billions of galaxies—we know that there is a lot of stuff. Therefore, we can conclude that this stuff creator has (had) the ability to create a lot of stuff. We can also look at the stuff of the universe and conclude that it took a lot of power to create all of that stuff. Obviously the stuff creator is (was) powerful.

A stuff creator who can create galaxies deserves my respect. When referring to someone I greatly respect I capitalize their title, such as when I refer to the President of the United States. Therefore, it is appropriate to refer with respect to the Stuff Creator.

It is difficult to conceive of a galaxy-creating Stuff Creator who could be killed or made to go out of existence. If there was some being or force powerful enough to kill the Stuff Creator or to make the Stuff Creator go out of existence, then that being or force would have god-like power, and hence, we would call that God. Therefore, we cannot get rid of God.

Of course, the Stuff Creator may have willed Himself[1] to die or go out of existence. That is a possibility. However, we have no evidence of that. Furthermore, the Stuff Creator must have had a purpose for creating the stuff—otherwise, He would not have created it. Since He had a purpose, He probably had an interest in creation. If He was interested, He probably would not have willed Himself out of existence. Therefore, it is reasonable for us to think that the Stuff Creator still exists.

Notice that I am saying, "It is reasonable to think." I am not saying (at this point) that we can prove that the Stuff Creator still exists. I am only saying that a reasonable person may use all of her or his logical abilities and come to believe that God exists now.

Inquiring minds do not stop at this point.

The reason Christians (and all theists) believe God exists now is not because they have taken a blind leap. It is because the existence of God is to them the most reasonable explanation for understanding the world as it is.

In 1998, Frank Sulloway and Michael Shermer surveyed 10,000 Americans, asking them, "Why do you believe in God?" The most common answers had to do with "good design," "natural beauty," "perfection," "complexity of the universe," and "experience of God in everyday life." All of these answers are based in reason.[2] A Christian who believes that God is alive today does not hold to this belief without evidence. In fact, if you talk to Christians about this subject, most of them will give you many examples of how God has indeed influenced their daily lives. To them, *this is evidence.*

Reason is what all people use to make conclusions about life, including those about God and religion. There is absolutely no justification to say that reason belongs only to the natural realm.

Christians should use all of their intellectual abilities, along with observation and testing, to reach the best possible decisions concerning truth—including religious truth. Only if people have examined the world around them and concluded that it is best explained with God as an element of the world, should they accept the existence of God. Furthermore, they should only embrace Christianity if they have come to understand that the Christian religion offers the best, most plausible explanation for the world around them.

All people use reason, and all people exercise faith. If we understand that believing is to invest one's life in what one has determined to be true, then we realize that all people believe in something. Whether they focus on the natural realm or the spiritual realm, they invest their lives in something, and that is faith.

Therefore, true faith (contrary to what the philosopher Kierkegaard taught) is *never* a blind leap.

Of course, there are some people who use faith as an excuse to be irresponsible. They say that they are going to trust God, when in reality they are simply living in denial. However, that is not true faith. That is a pseudo-faith. It is a lie. People who use true faith never make a blind leap. As I stated, they use all of their reasoning abilities and then invest their life in that which they have determined to be true.

Consider a Christian named Carl who is facing financial problems for which he has no solution. Carl is not worried but says he is going to trust God. To an onlooker it may appear that Carl is making a decision based on blind faith rather than reason. However, that is not true. The reason Carl is trusting God even though the circumstances in front of him seem impossible is because he has come to understand that God is faithful. Through many life experiences Carl has learned that God makes a way when there seems to be no way. Hence, Carl is using reason even though his situation seems impossible to the onlooker.

Compare this to Jane who cannot make the mortgage payment on her home. It is impossible for her to pay all of her bills, but she is not worried. To the onlooker it appears that Jane is being irresponsible (or blind). However, Jane knows something that the onlooker does not know. She knows that her father always comes by to visit her on the weekend, and if she has any financial needs, he helps out.

Neither Jane nor Carl is taking a blind leap of faith. Through experience and reason they know that someone will help them. Rather than worry, they have chosen to trust the one who has helped in the past. They are using reason and then placing their faith in someone.

The Truth

The point is that all people use faith and all people use reason. The biblical worldview recognizes that faith and reason are necessary for both realms. The biblical worldview is based in truth; it is the worldview that opens one's eyes to see truth.

With this understanding, we can reevaluate how Western thought erred so drastically in separating faith from reason. Earlier we mentioned that it was Soren Kierkegaard who argued that faith is always irrational. He gave the example of how God asked Abraham to kill his own son, and from this he argued that God requires us to hold beliefs that are ridiculous. In reality, Kierkegaard missed the primary lesson of Abraham offering his son to God. Abraham was not being blindly obedient. The most obvious message of the Abrahamic story is that he knew God.

Abraham had walked with God for many years. Before preparing his son Isaac for the sacrifice, Abraham confidently stated, *"God will provide for Himself the lamb for the burnt offering...."* (Gen. 22:8). Abraham knew that God would intervene. He knew that God would somehow provide a sacrifice or even raise Isaac from the dead if necessary. Therefore, he was not taking a blind leap of faith. Abraham was acting based on his knowledge of God.

The Truth

This reveals another fundamental aspect of the ancient Hebrew worldview: people can learn the ways of God and even know Him. This is a foundational and prominent theme throughout the Scriptures. In fact, aside from this theme, the Bible has very little to say to humanity. It is the central theme of Scripture, Judaism, and Christianity. Yes, people can know God.

Discussion Questions

1. What led you to a personal belief in God?

2. Would you say your belief is based on fact? Reason? Emotion? Knowledge?

3. What keeps you in relationship with God?

Chapter 13

TWO DIFFERENT FOUNDATIONS FOR OUR WORLDVIEW

W E HAVE IDENTIFIED the foundations of two different world-views: the worldview of those who wrote the Bible and the worldview of modern Western intellectualism.

The Worldview of Those Who Wrote the Bible

The Worldview of Modern Western Intellectualism

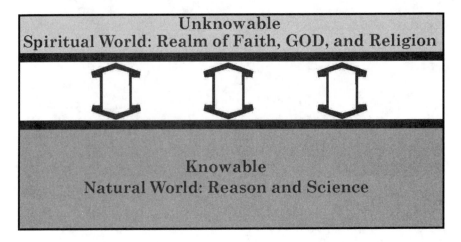

If we look at the world strictly through the eyes of Western intellectualism, God's existence cannot be proven because by definition we have placed God in the realm of the unknowable.

Compare the worldview of Western intellectualism to a computer that has been programmed to calculate that $2 + 2 = 5$. It does not matter how many times you run that summation, that computer will always come out with the incorrect answer of 5. In similar fashion, one's mind may be programmed to think that God, religion, and faith are of the spiritual realm, while science, reason, and knowledge are of the natural realm. It does not matter how many times that framework is imposed upon the facts, the answers will always come out that faith is unreasonable and God is unknowable.

Many agnostics will reason that if there is a God, then it is His responsibility to reveal Himself. Certainly a person cannot be expected to believe in something that cannot be seen or verified. Certainly if there is a God, He will not hold us accountable to believe in Him, since He is the one who is failing to make Himself known. It is His fault that we do not believe in Him—or so the agnostic reasons.

Yet, it is the Western worldview that blinds a person from seeing the reality of God. To see this more clearly, think again of the words we quoted earlier from the famous atheist Richard Dawkins: "Faith is the great cop-out, the great excuse to evade the need to think and evaluate evidence." Dawkins can only make this statement because he has assumed the worldview of modern Western intellectualism. However, if we hold to a worldview with no wall between the spiritual and natural realms, we could restructure Dawkins' words to state: "The worldview of modern Western intellectualism is the great cop-out, the great excuse to evade the need to think about God and evaluate evidence for His existence."

The truth is that any worldview that relegates things like God, religion, and faith to the spiritual world is a worldview built on an indefensible foundation. It may be attractive to people who want to distance themselves from facing reality, but it is tragic when modern-day Christians get pulled into that deceptive way of thinking.

Most Christians think that their worldview has been built on a biblical foundation. In reality, Western Christianity has a mixture of biblical thought and Western thought. It is most accurate to say that Western Christianity is the result of taking biblical truths and laying them upon the spiritual/natural division developed by the ancient Greek philosophers.

That division became more and more pronounced throughout the later part of the Middle Ages. As I mentioned earlier, theology and philosophy were king and queen in the kingdom of education. Much more than the Bible, Aristotle's writings were the focus of study. When discussing theology, students and professors spent most of their time dissecting and rehashing the writings of Church giants like Augustine and Thomas Aquinas—leaders who had developed their theology on the ancient Greek foundation.

When the historical Church went through the Scientific Revolution along with the rest of Western society, it was pulled right along and in many ways was at the forefront of change. The separation of the spiritual and natural worlds became even more clearly defined. Then God and faith were compartmentalized in the spiritual world while science and knowledge were compartmentalized in the natural world.

This compartmentalization was most prominent in philosophy. When philosophers such as Descartes, Hume, Kant, and Hegel developed their ideas, they each built on the spiritual/natural division. Even today Western philosophy is fully locked into the dichotomous worldview laid down by the ancient Greek philosophers.

Unfortunately, Christian theology developed side-by-side and intertwined with Western philosophy. Church leaders like Martin Luther and John Calvin were fully submerged in the Western dichotomy of the spiritual world versus the natural world. Of course, they did not limit God to the spiritual world, but they still were Western people with Western minds. It is disturbing for modern Christians to hear this, but in some ways, Plato and Aristotle have had a more profound impact upon Western Christianity than the apostle Paul (proven by the fact that most university-educated Christians today cannot agree with Paul that God's existence is undeniable and obvious).

There are many implications of this that we will discuss as we continue. Here we can simply mention how the foundation that divides the spiritual world from the natural world tends to create a lifestyle separated from the spiritual and supernatural. This is most obvious by considering a Western-minded atheist and then relating that to a modern Christian. Let me explain.

If God were to perform a miracle healing before a crowd of Western-minded atheists, they would make every attempt to give a natural explanation for the event. In their minds, natural events must have natural causes. Therefore, if God were to work a miraculous healing in their presence, thoughts would immediately go through their minds that the healing was not a true miracle but perhaps the result of coincidence, psychosomatic phenomenon, or deception. The modern Western mind can't help but impose such thoughts upon supernatural experiences. Because the framework through which they view life allows for no miracles, they must search for a natural explanation—and they usually find it.

This same process goes through the mind of Christians who have been indoctrinated in the Western worldview. They may want to believe, but their minds will mold the events to fit the split spiritual/ natural framework. Such patterns of thought go beyond our understanding of miracles and permeate all our understanding. They subtly create a lifestyle separated from the spiritual and supernatural. They lead to a form of godliness, but deny the power.

In Section II we will develop our worldview starting with no separation between the spiritual and natural realms. Having identified this error at the foundation of Western thought, we will now return to studying how the Western worldview continued developing on a faulty foundation.

Discussion Questions

1. How can we explain the tremendous influence of the Western Church, given that it rests on the flawed foundation of the ancient Greek spiritual/natural division?

2. Do you find your mind searching for spiritual causes for all natural phenomena?

Chapter 14

THEN CAME RATIONALISM
AND THE ENLIGHTENMENT

B UILDING ON THE FOUNDATION that the spiritual and natural
worlds are distinct and separate, the Scientific Revolution led people to conclude that the only truth that is available to humanity is that
which pertains to the natural world. Furthermore, the only way to discover this truth is through observation and testing. People came to
believe that if they simply apply their reasoning abilities to understand
that which is observed, then they will obtain truth.

This way of thinking was, in part, a reaction to the beliefs of the
Middle Ages when so many people blindly accepted what the established Church taught. The Church claimed to have revelation from God
that needed no testing or verification. The Scientific Revolution dis-
missed that claim as foolishness. Further, they built their worldview
with the assumption that God is not involved with this natural world.

Indeed, people in the Middle Ages were gullible—at least from our
modern-day perspective. They needed to look more critically at many of
the things they had been taught. However, to deny the possibility of
God being involved in this world was a huge, unjustifiable leap. Once
people took that leap, they continued down a path leading farther and
farther away from God.

Soon after thinkers decided that the natural world is understandable through the scientific method of observation and testing, they applied that method to every area of life. Leaders engaged their reasoning powers to learn the principles that govern politics, economics, education, human behavior, and many other fields of study. This became known as "Rationalism."

As the Western world moved from the Scientific Revolution into Rationalism, people were left in a material universe with either a God who is uninvolved in this world or no God at all. The resulting change in Western society has been called the "Enlightenment," a term that implies that humanity came out of darkness and into a new understanding of reality.

Rationalism and the Enlightenment

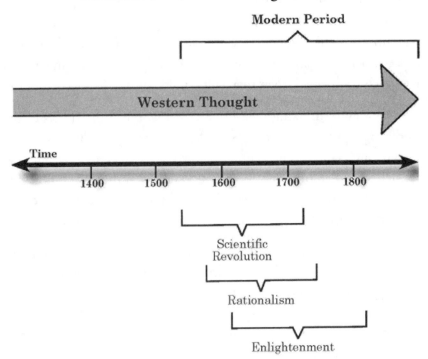

The thoughts of over 100 Enlightenment thinkers were compiled in a 28-volume work called *The Encyclopedia* (published in 1751). The French philosopher Voltaire (1694-1778) was the most influential thinker of that period. Further developing the thoughts of the Enlightenment were thinkers such as Rousseau (1712-1778) and David Hume (1711-1776).

During the Enlightenment, much thought was given to the nature of humanity. Philosophers developed the concept of man's dignity and worth. They also concluded that humanity is inherently good, and therefore, if people are allowed to be free, they will naturally produce good things.

This Enlightenment thought lies at the foundation of our modern Western educational system. The positive view of humanity led leaders to conclude that education is the answer to the world's problems. If good people simply have the right information, then they will produce good in the world. This idea also led to the idea that people must be liberated from institutions such as government and religion, which suppress human expression. It was believed that society must be restructured to liberate humanity so the world could become a wonderful, harmonious place.

With Enlightenment thought during the late 1700s, there was much discussion of democratic societies. Since humanity is good, people must be free to govern themselves and allow the good within them to arise. No longer could hierarchical monarchies be allowed to rule. Fixed social classes could not be tolerated. Calling for these changes in society, the Enlightenment ushered in the Democratic Revolution.

This worldview was at the foundation of the American Revolution (1775-1783) and the French Revolution (1789-1799). However, historians typically will explain that the American Constitution reveals a mixture of Enlightenment thought with the historical Church's concept of humanity. Hence, the optimistic U.S. Constitution incorporated checks and balances to ensure protection from the wickedness of which humanity is capable.

As the U.S. Constitution shows a mixture of Enlightenment thought and Augustinian thought, so also most people in the Western world hold to a similar mixture. Of course, there are diehard Enlightenment thinkers among Western intellectuals, and there are diehard Augustinian thinkers among fundamental Christians, but most people fall somewhere between the two extremes and they frequently vacillate back and forth.

Now step back and notice how Enlightenment thought was diametrically opposed to the three fundamentals (discussed in Chapter 5) that Augustine played a key role in establishing in the view of the historical Church.

	View of the Historic Church	View of the Enlightenment
I. God	In Control	Not Involved
II. Humanity	Inherently Evil	Inherently Good
III. World	Corrupt in Its Fallen State	Wonderful in Its Natural State

On the above chart, I have added to our list a distinction pertaining to how they each viewed the natural world. Augustine, and those who followed in his footsteps, saw the world as corrupt because of the fall of Adam. The Enlightenment thinkers focused on a different aspect of the world. Writers such as Henry David Thoreau (1817-1862) championed the idea of how wonderful the world is *in its natural condition*. This became the common view embraced by Enlightened thinkers.

Even though the historical Church leaders emphasized the world *in its fallen state* and the leaders of the Enlightenment emphasized the world *in its natural state,* they were talking about the same world: the mountains, trees, lakes, wildlife, and everything being referred to when we speak of nature. The leaders of the Church and the Enlightenment focused on different aspects of nature and came to very different conclusions about the nature of nature.

In Section II we will develop the proper Christian view on these and related subjects, but for now we need to see where Enlightenment thought has taken the modern world.

Discussion Questions

1. Having read the views of the historical Church and the Enlightenment thinkers, what are your views concerning God's control of this world?

2. How have your views been influenced by the polar thinking of the historical Church and Enlightenment thinkers?

Chapter 15

RATIONALISM UNDERMINING CHRISTIANITY

ADVOCATES OF THE ENLIGHTENMENT do not believe in miracles. As God was moved farther and farther away from involvement in this world, His influence became unrecognizable. In the mind of the "Enlightened" person, this world is one of reason and science.

The Enlightened Worldview

**The Real World Is the
World of Reason and Science**

As this worldview was applied to all areas of life, the Bible soon came into its sights. Enlightened Bible scholars attempted to explain the Holy Book as a book that had been written by simple-minded people explaining what they observed through their prescientific worldview. Hence, modern Enlightened scholars dissected the Bible and attempted to explain "what really happened."

For example, a common explanation for the Bible's report of Jesus multiplying bread and fish in order to feed 4,000 people (see Mark 8:1-9) goes like this. Thousands of people were following this leader named Jesus, and one day He inspired a "giving spirit" within the listeners. As a consequence, they each took out the food they were carrying with them and they shared it with one another. Hence, Jesus fed the 4,000, not through a miracle but through His charismatic abilities.

With a similar approach, Enlightened thinkers analyzed and reinterpreted the entire New Testament. Thomas Jefferson, the United States president most known for his Enlightenment thought, took his New Testament and cut out every passage that did not fit into the rationalist's understanding. He then had printed his own version of the New Testament without the miraculous elements such as the virgin birth and resurrection of Jesus. Like many leaders of the period, he reduced the Bible to a book of morals with little to no historical value.

Such dissecting and reinterpreting of the Bible became known as *higher criticism* and gave birth to *liberal theology*. Liberal theologians (I am speaking of those liberal in their theology, not their political views) imposed the rationalist's worldview upon the Bible, discarding or explaining away anything that does not measure up to their litmus test of being explainable in accordance with natural laws.

According to liberal theologians, this world is a world of reason, and hence, there is no such thing as prophecy, for no one can really know the future. With this understanding, liberal theologians used their reasoning ability to explain how the Book of Daniel could report about three kingdoms yet to come in the future: the Medo-Persian Empire, the Greek Empire, and the Roman Empire (see Dan. 2, 8). Since it was impossible for Daniel to have known of these future empires, the book with his name must have been written by some unknown author who lived after the three empires. That unknown author must have then placed the name of Daniel on his writings to give credence to his message. As a consequence, liberal theologians started to refer to the author of the Book of Daniel as "Pseudo-Daniel" (meaning, "false Daniel").

With this pattern of thought, they began redating any book of the Bible that offered prophecies of the future. They began confidently asserting that the leaders once thought to be the authors of those books certainly could not have written them since the real authors must have lived after the "prophesied events." Hence, there were many pseudo-authors.

This process of renaming and redating various books was most evident in the liberal teachers' dealing with the Book of Isaiah. The reason Isaiah was so key is because there are numerous prophecies pertaining to a coming Messiah, and those prophecies were amazingly fulfilled in Jesus Christ. Therefore, liberals decided that the Messianic prophecies in Isaiah (especially the last half of the book) must have been added by some unknown Christian scribe after Jesus lived.

Most of the proposed manipulation of the written records was proven to be foolishness when the Dead Sea Scrolls were found in 1947. Among those texts were found several copies of the complete Old Testament (except the Book of Esther), which date before 150 B.C. Knowing this, any researcher with integrity must admit that most of the events prophesied in the Old Testament were written long before the prophesied events were fulfilled.

In spite of this, liberal theologians continue today to impose their worldview upon the New Testament. As for the Gospels, which propose to report the life of Jesus, the liberal theologians typically say that those Gospels were not really written by the apostles but rather by leaders who lived several generations after Jesus lived. By that time, the early Church had so made a legend of this man called Jesus that miracles, prophecy, and even rising from the dead were accredited to Him. Obviously, according to the liberal theologians, none of these reports were factual.

Since the start of the 20th century, liberal theologians have arisen to dominate the religious departments of our secular universities (and many colleges and seminaries that claim to be Christian). Today there is a mass of teaching material that has been produced from the liberal understanding of Scripture. In liberal circles, the definition of a "Bible scholar" is not someone who has spent years studying the Bible, but it is someone who has applied rationalism to the understanding of religion. So when liberal teachers of religion today refer to "Bible scholars," they are not referring to the tens of thousands of pastors or professors who teach in our churches and Bible colleges actually believing what the Bible says. When a liberal professor makes a statement such as, "Bible scholars agree that...," they are referring to educated teachers who think like themselves. Unfortunately, when naïve listeners hear about the topics of which "Bible scholars" agree, they tend to accept those views as true. I hope you can see how it is a circular (and deceptive) way of communication.

Another term often used by liberal professors in a deceptive fashion is the word, "critical." Of course, we need to think critically in the sense of questioning the ideas being taught to us. However, students sitting in university classrooms are usually guided to focus on and find fault in those ideas that are contrary to the professors' own beliefs—ideas that are typically valued by tradition and religion. As a result, critical thinking is typically the process through which students are led to reject the values of their parents and religious upbringing.

In modern liberal religion classes there is much talk about "searching for the historical Jesus." Since the liberal teachers have already decided that there is no such thing as the miraculous, they attempt to extract from the written records of the life of Jesus what "really happened." After being critical of and then removing the miraculous elements, they are left with a belief in a real historical human being who lived in the Middle East during the first century, but who had been made a legendary figure by the generations who lived after Him.[1] By separating the mythical from the historical, liberal scholars believe they have a more accurate picture of who this Jesus really was.[2]

In modern universities that have classes focusing on "the historical Jesus," students are taught that the man Jesus who lived in the first century was a mythological figure. He truly lived, but He was just a man. When students enroll in a class entitled *Bible as Literature,* they may expect to get an opportunity to read the Bible, but if the course is taught by a liberal professor, they will not even need a Bible. Instead, they will learn and then be tested on their ability to understand the Bible as literature—in the same sense as Homer's *Iliad* and *Odyssey* are literature, filled with mythology. When students sit in a religion class taught by a liberal professor, their minds are being formed to see Jesus and the Bible through the lens of rationalism. The supernatural is explained away, and the spiritual side of reality is denied.

It is not only young college students who are often shaken in their beliefs by liberal theology teachers. Thousands of adults have entered liberal seminaries (not all seminaries are liberal) with hopes of serving God in ministerial positions, only to come out of those seminaries doubting even the existence of God. Countless numbers of pastors and priests already serving in churches have dedicated personal time to study the writings of certain liberal writers only to drift away from the very beliefs that first led them into the ministry. Along with some of my friends I include myself in this group. A seminary I attended over 30 years ago was especially hard on me, and it took me several years to rebuild a solid biblical worldview.

Discussion Questions

1. Is it possible to live the Christian life, accepting what Jesus stood for, while doubting the literal accuracy of the Gospels?

2. What difference does your level of literal belief in the Gospels make, if any, in your Christian life?

3. Can you think of any book that we should take more seriously than the Bible?

Chapter 16

CASTING DOUBTS UPON SCRIPTURE

THE ENLIGHTENED WORLDVIEW lies at the foundation of most of our secular institutions of higher learning today. Although all people in the Western world are influenced by it, it is the students at our secular universities (and some Christian universities) who are subject to a constant bombardment of Enlightenment thought. Every field of study molds the student's mind to see truth as only that which can be observed and tested—as the rationalist sees it.

I am being critical, but I do not want to be completely derogatory of the whole Western educational system. Education is a doorway to wonderful opportunities. Teachers are gifts from God, and Christian teachers are positioned throughout our secular schools. However, the influence of Christianity decreases as we move up into the higher levels of education. Modern universities are seedbeds of doubt concerning the beliefs of one's parents and forefathers. There are also forceful attacks upon previous religious training, and liberal professors are especially hostile toward Evangelical Christianity.

The first two years of university training are particularly destructive to Christian beliefs. This is true because new students are at a vulnerable time of life: leaving the security of their home environment, enjoying freedom from their parents, being very idealistic, and eagerly hoping to see the world through new eyes. Although we may not want to admit it, another factor in making young adults vulnerable is the fact that hormone levels are at their highest, and with sexual opportunities increased, many are eager to embrace a worldview that makes it easy to rationalize sexual promiscuity. Add into this picture idealistic college teachers who want to influence the minds of youth, and enjoy the turbulence that can be created in the classroom.

In many university environments the Christian faith is made to look ridiculous. As mentioned earlier, liberal professors teach or imply that the Bible was written by naïve people who were trying to explain things through their prescientific worldview. There are two accusations repeatedly put forth to show the ridiculousness of those who believe the Bible.

First, liberal professors will often say, "The Bible teaches that the earth is flat." In reality, there is no passage in the Bible that states or implies that the earth is flat. In fact, the Bible is the only ancient book known to teach that the world is a sphere. For example, Isaiah 40:22 speaks of the *"circle of the earth,"* but scholars know that the original Hebrew word translated as *circle* is accurately translated as *sphere*. While many of the surrounding cultures in ancient times believed that the earth was supported on the back of a huge turtle, Job praised God declaring that God *"hangs the earth on nothing"* (Job 26:7).

Modern liberal professors like to ridicule Bible-believing Christians by associating them with the medieval Church and then saying things like, "The Church believed the earth was flat." In reality, educated Christians in medieval times (and even educated Greeks in the ancient world) commonly thought the world was round. It was common knowledge that the hull of a ship sailing away disappears before the sails do. Most educated people also knew that the earth casts a circular shadow on the moon during an eclipse. Dante's writings, which were among the most popular of all among medieval Christianity, assumed the idea of a spherical earth.

It is also worth noting that Christopher Columbus (1451-1506) believed he had a divine mission to accomplish, and his belief that the earth was a sphere was profoundly influenced by two Christian works: Pope Pius II's *Historia Rerum ubique Gestarum,* published in 1477, and Cardinal Pierre d'Ally's *Imago Mundi,* published in the early 1480s (when Copernicus was just a child and Galileo wasn't even born).

The second erroneous accusation that is often raised by liberal professors to undermine students' belief in the Bible goes like this: "The Bible taught that the sun revolved around the earth." When we look at this accusation more carefully we find that it too is pure foolishness.

We know that most people in the Middle Ages thought that the sun revolved around the earth, but this belief was seated into Western civilization primarily through the work of the Greek astronomer Ptolemy and the philosopher Aristotle. Even though many medieval church leaders clung to this "Ptolemaic" understanding of the solar system, it is nowhere in the Bible.

Some teachers in the Middle Ages referred to Joshua chapter 10, which tells us that Joshua prayed and the sun stood still. This was taken by some to be biblical proof that the sun revolves around the earth. In reality, today we know that all movement is relative to the position of the observer. For example, if you look up at the clouds you may notice that they are moving; but in reality it may be you who is moving as the earth rotates. To be scientifically accurate we would have to say that the clouds are moving relative to you. Or we could say that you are moving relative to the clouds. Both statements are equally true. Similarly, it is scientifically accurate to say that the sun is moving relative to the earth or the earth is moving relative to the sun.

With a similar perspective we must look at the passages in the Bible that refer to the sun rising and setting (e.g., Eccles. 1:5). These do not mean that the sun revolves around the earth. Even today our weather forecasters on television announce when the sun will rise and set, but we do not accuse them of believing that the sun revolves around the earth. It is scientifically accurate to talk about the sun rising and setting so long as we are speaking about it relative to our perspective on earth.

In pointing this out I am defending the Bible's accuracy, but I do not want to imply that the Bible was written to be a scientific textbook. It was written to teach people about God and His relationship with humanity.

There are many other fronts on which the Bible is attacked. Students taking a religion course are likely at some point to be given a list of proposed contradictions in the Bible. Of course, these are not presented as "proposed" contradictions, but are offered as proof that the Bible was written by prescientific humans who cannot be trusted.

The liberal professor will typically offer a list of approximately 100 "mistakes in the Bible." One of the most well-known "mistakes" has to do with the two different accounts of how Judas, the traitor, died. In Acts 1:18 we are told:

> ...and falling headlong, he burst open in the middle and all his intestines gushed out.

The other account is in the Gospel of Matthew:

> ...and he went away and hanged himself (Matthew 27:5).

For someone looking for contradictions, indeed, these two differing accounts of Judas' death might be convincing.

110

On the other hand, some Bible colleges and seminaries offer courses to explain the proposed contradictions of the Bible. This one is easily explained once a student knows the law of the Jewish people, that an unclean body (a dead body) may not be touched. Therefore, it is easy to understand that if Judas hung himself, his body would have remained hanging until it fell of its own accord after rotting to the point where it fell and the bowels gushed forth.

Of course, the student at the secular university is not offered the opposing arguments of how the apparent contradictions may be explained. Nor does the average student have the time to research those opposing arguments because universities provide a full course of study leaving little room for serious thoughts contrary to the professor's worldview. We could go on to discuss other proposed contradictions, but many other more qualified teachers have written on this subject.

In reality, the entire discussion concerning whether or not the Bible should be taken literally is an argument founded in the Western worldview. It is the Western mind that focuses on things being literally—scientifically—accurate or not. Of course, this discussion may be worth having because people want to know if the Bible is trustworthy. However, the often repeated saying, "whoever frames the argument, wins the argument" is applicable here. Let me explain.

The most important question is not whether we should take the Bible literally, but should we take it *seriously?* The question about literal accuracy should not even be considered until we first settle the issue concerning how seriously we should take the Bible.

To see this, all we have to do is realize that in the Bible we have over 2,000 years of documentation concerning the thoughts of various individuals and their understanding of the ways of God. Contributing to those thoughts are some of the most influential people in human history, such as Abraham, Isaac, Jacob, Moses, Samuel, Elijah, David,

Solomon, Isaiah, Daniel, Matthew, Mark, Luke, John, Paul, and Jesus. Their understanding of God has been preserved and passed on to us so successfully that today it is the book in more homes and hearts than any other book in human history. Should we take that book seriously? Of course! We would be foolish not to.

Let me say again that the Westerner's question concerning whether or not the Bible should be taken literally is a valid question. However, that question must not be allowed to push aside the more important question: "Should we take the Bible seriously?" Compare this to how we should take the U.S. Constitution seriously. There is no doubt that we should study and carefully value the U.S. Constitution simply because it is the foundation for the U.S. government and the 300 million people who live under its laws. Similarly, the Bible is the foundation for the largest religion in the world. More than *2 billion* people see it as the foundation of their lives. Should we take the Bible seriously? We would be foolish not to since it is the one book that is read and valued by more people than any other book in the world.

Yet, the vast majority of new students who enter our modern universities as churchgoers will emerge having no association with any church and questioning whether or not the Bible has anything valid to say to modern society. For people like myself who believe that going to church is a good thing and that the Bible is the most important written treasure available to humanity, we must conclude that our universities are tragically flawed. For example, think of a university as an auto mechanic who is being sent many cars to work on. If most of the cars come out of his shop more dysfunctional than when they went in, then we can reasonably conclude that something is wrong with that mechanic.

This may be no big deal for a Western-minded person who believes that religion is unprovable and God is unknowable, but for a person without the faith/reason dichotomy imposed upon the world, many facts about God and religion are provable and knowable. If education is about learning truth, then any education that leads students to abandon truth concerning God, religion, and the spiritual aspects of reality is seriously flawed.

I propose that we Christians who send our young adults into the modern secular universities, first prepare them by thoroughly discussing the very issues that we are discussing in these pages. Before the liberal professor teaches "the Bible as literature," let's explain how the Bible writers were recording their interactions with God. Perhaps they will remember this when the professor is comparing such sacred interactions with Homer's mythological adventures.[1]

Before the professor hands them a list of mistakes in the Bible, let's give them a list of the 300 or more prophecies in the Bible that have been fulfilled. Perhaps then our young adults will remember these fulfilled prophecies when the professor starts redating Bible books to later periods.

Students also need to be prepared when a liberal professor begins to talk about Jesus as if He simply was a leader who was made into a legendary figure three to six generations after He actually lived. When the professor tries to make this point by declaring that the New Testament books probably were not written until 100 or 200 years later, the students need to be armed with the truth. The apostle Paul, who wrote more than any other New Testament writer, was martyred in Rome under the reign of Nero in A.D. 68; therefore, his letters had to have been written within a short time after the death of Jesus.

We also have proof that the rest of the New Testament was written in the first century, because the Church fathers who lived in the first and second centuries (Clement, Barnabus, Polycarp, the writer of the *Didache,* Ignatius, Irenaeus, and Tertullian, along with many others) quoted within their own writings *several thousand passages* from the New Testament writings—which tells us that the New Testament was written before their times and it was already considered authoritative.

Finally, it is worth noting that the historical writings from the period tell us that every book that was placed in the New Testament was chosen to be included because it was either written by one of Jesus' apostles or it was written by a disciple under the direct tutelage of an apostle.[2]

Discussion Questions

1. If something cannot be proven scientifically, can it still be true? Should it be held as truth?

2. If you had a child preparing to leave home for college, how might you prepare them for the challenge against their Christian beliefs?

3. How successful do you think your preparations would be at protecting your child's beliefs?

Chapter 17

DIVERGENT PATHS OF THE WESTERN WORLDVIEW

LET'S TURN our attention back to the historical development of Western thought. We have seen two widely divergent paths: that of the historical Church and that of the Enlightenment.

Widely Divergent Paths of Western Thought

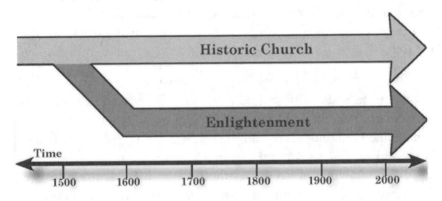

We have the historical Church (profoundly influenced by Augustine) concluding that God is in control of all things, people are inherently evil, and this world is corrupt because of Adam's sin. On the other hand, we have Enlightened thinkers concluding that God is not involved in this world, people are good, and this world is wonderful in

115

its natural state. We can also add to our list what we learned about the Scientific Revolution, and the claim of some adherents that God's existence is unprovable and He is unknowable. This understanding is part of the Enlightened worldview.

	View of the Historic Church	View of the Enlightenment
I. God	In Control	Not Involved Unproveable Unknowable
II. Humanity	Inherently Evil	Inherently Good
III. World	Corrupt in Its Fallen State	Wonderful in Its Natural State

During the Protestant Reformation of the 16th century, several million people left Roman Catholicism. Before that time, the terminology "historical Church" referred to the Roman Catholic Church (and to those in the East, the Orthodox Church). After the Protestant Reformation, a multitude of denominations emerged, and all of them that held to the historical faith in Jesus can be included in the label "historical Church."

Two of the strongest branches within Protestantism were Lutheranism and Reformed Christianity. Both of these Protestant groups continued to hold to the three points of Augustinian thought concerning God, humanity, and the world. Martin Luther, the father of Lutheranism, was an Augustinian monk before he took his bold stand against the teaching of Roman Catholicism. John Calvin, the father of Reformed theology, taught that God is in control of all things, people are totally depraved, and this world is corrupt because of Adam's sin.

While Reformed theology (Calvinism) has held tightly to the three points of Augustinian thought that we have been discussing, the rest of the historical Church has been influenced in various measures by Enlightenment thought. As a consequence, the views of the historical

Church now span the spectrum from Reformed theology to Enlightenment thought, which I attempt to show in the diagram below.

The Broadened Views of the Historical Church

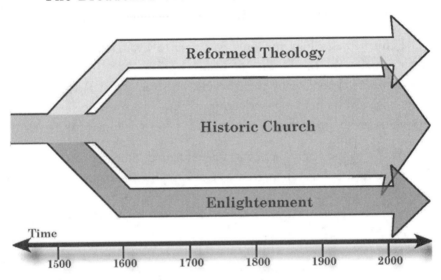

The thoughts of Reformed theology have always been at great variance with Enlightenment thought. Therefore, in the diagram above I placed Reformed theology opposite from Enlightenment thought. I also placed Reformed theology as distinct from the historical Church, but I do not mean to imply that adherents of Reformed theology are separate from the historical Church. They should be thought of as part of the historical Church. However, their beliefs are more strictly defined than much of the historical Church. In fact, many Christians who are in the Reformed tradition would not consider anyone outside of their viewpoint as true Christians. They would certainly doubt the sincerity of any members of the historical Church who lean strongly toward Enlightenment thought.

Reformed theology gave rise to modern Evangelicalism. The word "Evangelical" is used differently in different parts of the world. In most

117

of Europe, it refers to all Protestant churches and Protestant Christians. In North America, it refers to Protestant churches and Christians who emphasize evangelism and the need for a personal commitment to Jesus Christ. I will be using this second definition. (I am including Charismatics and Pentecostals within this category of Evangelicals.)

Reformed theology not only gave rise to Evangelical Christianity, but it remains the big brother of Evangelicalism. Modern Evangelicals have some diversity among their beliefs, but teachers of Reformed theology have always held a prominent position within Evangelical circles, serving as an anchor, tethering Evangelicals to their historical roots.

As Evangelicalism grew out of Reformed thought, our modern Western educational system grew out of Enlightenment thought.

Evangelicalism Versus Western Education

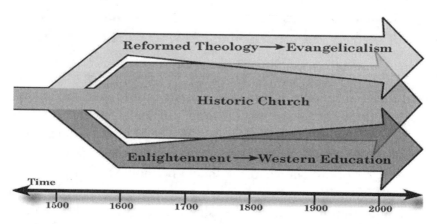

As we discussed earlier, liberal professors in our secular universities are often antagonistic toward Christianity. They tend to portray today's Evangelical Christians as naïve, uninformed people still holding to the same superstitions as church-going people did in the Middle Ages. They enjoy talking about the foolish judgments that the Roman Catholic Church made against 16th- and 17th-century scientists; and then they tend to put all Christians into the same category responsible for those mistakes. They like to think of themselves as the product of the Scientific Revolution while Christianity totally missed out.

Because these accusations are made so frequently and are often overblown, allow me to take the next chapter to diffuse a few of those that are based on misunderstandings and myth.

Discussion Questions

1. Given the discussion of the three worldviews: Evangelicalism, the Historical Church, and Western Education—can you identify and discuss their influences on your personal belief system?

2. Can you see the influence of Enlightenment thought on your education?

Chapter 18

THE CHURCH AND SCIENCE

THOSE WHO are antagonistic toward Christianity often portray the Church as opposed to science. They like to talk about the foolish judgments that the medieval Church made toward the first scientists. Indeed, the Church did make mistakes, but liberals (again, I am referring to those liberal in their theological beliefs) and atheists often exaggerate those mistakes to the point of rewriting history.

Contrary to how liberal professors like to portray the Scientific Revolution of the 16th century, it was not a battle between the Church and the scientific world. It was first and foremost a battle between the fathers of science (leaders such as Copernicus, Galileo, Newton, and Bacon) and the scholastics of the universities.[1] Those scholastics were not clinging to ideas based in the Bible, but rather ideas based in ancient Greek thought.

As we mentioned earlier, the idea of the sun revolving around the earth was seated into Western civilization through the work of the Greek astronomer Ptolemy and the philosopher Aristotle. Even though many medieval Church leaders clung to this Ptolemaic understanding of the solar system, it is nowhere in the Bible. We also know that it was Plato's teaching that planets must revolve in perfectly circular motions that hindered Copernicus and others from even considering the possibility that planetary orbits might be elliptical, not circular. In subjects such as these, the pursuit of truth was hindered primarily by the ancient Greek worldview.

The leaders of the Scientific Revolution were theists, and some were even Church leaders. Copernicus was a canon—a church official of a cathedral in the region now known as Poland. Galileo received his early education in a monastery, and the foundation of his teaching was his belief that God had given two books of revelation: the book of nature and the book of Scripture. Although Isaac Newton did not believe in the Trinity, he wrote just as much about theology as he did about science. Francis Bacon had great disagreements with the Church, but he was a religious man, writing treatises on the Psalms and prayer. Bacon also made it clear that he desired people to have true knowledge of nature so that the Creator of nature may be worshiped.

Rather than talk about these fathers of science being devout theists, modern people who are antagonistic toward Christianity like to portray them as being in opposition to the Church. Most often exaggerated are the stories about how difficult it was for Copernicus and Galileo to promote their ideas. Carl Sagan describes Galileo "in a Catholic dungeon threatened with torture." Sam Harris tells his readers about the Church's practice of "torturing scholars to the point of madness for merely speculating about the stars."[2] These and other atheists have drawn pictures in the minds of listeners that the Church was torturing and killing any scientist who openly challenged the current beliefs of the Church. Others parroted these stories and embellished them to the point where they no longer knew where truth ended and storytelling began.

In reality, before publishing his controversial book, *On the Revolution of the Celestial Spheres,* Copernicus presented his ideas in a lecture at the Vatican attended by Pope Clement VII and several cardinals. Cardinal Nicholas von Schönberg wrote to Copernicus urging him to publish his book, and that letter was included in his book.

Copernicus respectfully dedicated to the pope his book about the earth revolving around the sun. Copernicus was never persecuted by the Roman Catholic Church for his ideas, and in fact, his book was not even published until after his death in 1543. The Roman Catholic Church basically ignored his work until the 17th century, but a few leaders of the Protestant churches (most notably, Lutherans) spoke out against Copernicus' ideas.[3]

When Galileo came into the spotlight, he was admired by Pope Gregory XV. Galileo went to Rome in 1616, and he was met with great fanfare. He was, in fact, a celebrity. He stayed in the grand Medici villa, met with Pope Gregory XV more than once, and attended several receptions hosted by various bishops and cardinals. When Pope Gregory was replaced by Cardinal Barberini (renamed Pope Urban VIII), Galileo was pleased because he knew that, as cardinal, Barberini had been a supporter of scientific research. Barberini was also a fan of Galileo and even wrote a poem eulogizing him. When Galileo first published his writings about the earth revolving around the sun, they were quickly accepted by many Jesuit astronomers but rejected by rival academics who wanted the Church to intervene.[4]

In 1633 Galileo stood trial before an Inquisition, but he was never charged with heresy. He was reprimanded primarily because he violated an earlier promise that he had made to only teach as hypothesis the idea of the earth revolving around the sun. Galileo was also careless in some of his research and in the communication of his ideas. Contrary to what some modern pseudohistorians like to say, Galileo was never placed in a dungeon or tortured. There may have been a threat of torture, but he was ordered to recant—which he did—and then was released into the care of the archbishop of Siena who hosted him for five months in his palace. After that he was allowed to return to his own villa in Florence, where he was supposed to be under house arrest, though he still ventured out to visit his daughters.[5]

Other than the incident with Galileo—which is severely exaggerated by modern liberals—there is no historical record of the Church ever condemning a scientific theory.[6]

The idea of the Church getting involved in matters of science seems strange to the modern mind, but we must understand the culture of that period. For Church leaders to investigate certain scientific advancements was not some strange practice, nor was it an unreasonable exercise of their authority. During the Middle Ages, most universities and places of scientific research were supported by the Church. The vast majority of literate people in Europe were part of the clergy. They were the authorities, not because they were religious, but primarily because they were educated. Before the Protestant Reformation, the whole of Europe looked to the Roman Catholic Church to put its stamp of approval on all fields of study.

Of course, certain Church leaders made some foolish decisions in the 16th and 17th centuries, but it had made thousands of decisions for the benefit of humanity. The Roman Catholic Church had been a stabilizing influence for over 1,000 years throughout Europe. Hence, it is a distortion of history to talk only about the foolish decisions that the Church made.

Contrary to what liberal professors like to state or imply, the Church did more for Western science than any other institution. For many centuries, monasteries were the only place dedicated to the preservation of written knowledge. In the Middle Ages, most universities, medical research institutions, and observatories were Church sponsored. Even in modern times, the Church has been very involved with education and research. Harvard, Yale, Northwestern, Princeton, Dartmouth, and Brown all began as Christian institutions.

Among the many Christian leaders who made great contributions to the development of early science were Copernicus, Kepler, Galileo,

Brahe, Descartes, Boyle, Newton, Leibniz, Gassendi, Pascal, Mersenne, Cuvier, Harvey, Dalton, Faraday, Herschel, Joule, Lyell, Lavoisier, Priestley, Kelvin, Ohm, Ampere, Steno, Pasteur, Maxwell, Planck, and Mendell. All of these men were church leaders, some were clergymen, and Georges Lemaitre, who first proposed the "big bang" theory, was a priest.[7]

These facts are overlooked by liberal professors today who want to place Christianity in a bad light. They like to rehearse the negative aspects of the medieval Church and then subtly bring today's Christians into the same picture. The truth is that most of today's Evangelicals would like to distance themselves from the medieval Roman Catholic Church just as much as Enlightened thinkers distance themselves. Unfortunately, they get thrown into the same group by people antagonistic toward Christianity.

Evangelicals have their own actions for which they must answer. Since the end of the 19th century, a significant portion of Evangelical Christians have opposed the teaching of Darwin's theory of evolution. However, it would be inaccurate to say that Christianity as a whole rejected Darwin's theories. He was, in fact, honored by the Church in England, being buried in Westminster Abbey where his remains (along with Isaac Newton's) still lie today. Henry Ward Beecher (1813-1887), probably the most famous and influential American preacher of his time wrote a book entitled *Evolution and Religion,* which strongly supported evolutionary thought.

Today, some conservative Evangelicals continue to distance themselves from certain fields of science.[8] However, the largest percentage of Evangelicals (and Roman Catholics[9]) have in various ways synchronized their religious beliefs with current scientific discovery. The truth is that Christian leaders are intensely engaged in the issues of our time. This includes every field of science. Furthermore, Christians are thoroughly involved throughout the various fields of science, and their presence increases every year.[10]

Discussion Questions

1. What have you been taught concerning the influence of the historical Church on humanity's scientific advancement? Has this chapter altered your views? If so, how?

2. In what ways have you synchronized your religious beliefs with current scientific discovery?

Chapter 19

THE ADVANCEMENT OF SOCIETY

A S AN OUTCOME of the Scientific Revolution, secular people began to push God out of their consciousness and to believe that their destiny was in their own hands. The Enlightenment led people to believe that the world will become a more and more wonderful place as people are educated and released from oppression. This optimism was developed and furthered by many leaders and thinkers—too many to discuss in a brief overview such as this.

There is, however, one philosopher worth drawing our attention to: Georg Wilhelm Friedrich Hegel (1770-1831). As a professor of philosophy in Germany, Hegel offered a way of viewing the people of different nations as in a constant state of development and struggle. He taught that every people group attempts to solve the problems facing them but in every advancement there are inherent problems. Hence, the next generations will attempt to confront those inherent problems and replace them with a way of thinking that both advances society and creates problems of its own. As a result, the people of every nation advance, but it is through the back and forth struggles—often violent struggles— between nations.

Hegel's understanding of society's advancement is often summarized by saying: "first comes a thesis, then an antithesis, followed by a synthesis." This means that people develop an answer to their problems (thesis);

then a few years later, people identify the resulting problems and attempt to correct them with their own answers (antithesis); in time, people merge the thesis and antithesis, coming up with a synthesis.

Every Society Is Advancing Through Back-and-Forth Struggles

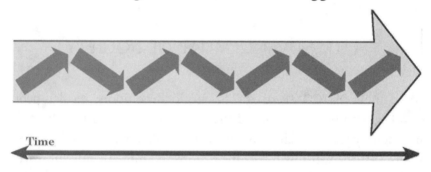

Time

Hegel's view of society has had a profound impact upon the Western mind. Most importantly, people have come to believe that society is moving in a positive direction, getting better and better. This understanding corresponded well with the ideas of evolutionary thought that were forming during the same period in history.

Although we will not be discussing it further, let me briefly point out that Karl Marx built on Hegel's understanding, but he identified the primary struggles as between classes of people within a nation. From this he developed the foundation for atheistic communism.

People in the Western world who accepted Hegel's views became comfortable with tension between opposing views. Because they saw society in a continual process—thesis, antithesis, and synthesis—no one is ever totally right. In other words, there is truth in the thesis and there is truth in the antithesis. Since no one has full truth, we must endeavor to hold other views as just as valid as our own. This understanding went hand-in-hand with a relativism that was also developing in Western society during the same period.

Relativism became an element of Enlightenment thought, while the idea of advancing society was both an element of Enlightenment thought and Christian thought. In fact, the historical Church had a more profound impact in forming this idea of advancing society than Hegel did. Please let me explain.

New thoughts never arise in a vacuum. Since ancient times, Hebrew thought was always one of seeing time as moving forward. This was in contrast to most civilizations in ancient times, including Greek, which saw human history as cyclical, alternating between stages of hope and despair, growth and decay. Rather than seeing society advancing, they envisioned humanity repeating the same patterns over and over again in a very fatalistic manner. In his excellent book *Christ and Time,* Oscar Cullmann explains how ancient Hebrew and early Christianity saw time moving in a linear, progressive manner.[1] This understanding is the foundation of our modern idea of society advancing. In order to see society in this fashion, leaders in the Western world had to overcome the ancient Greek thought patterns. This triumph of Hebrew thought over Greek thought did not fully emerge until the 17th and 18th centuries.

The historical Church played the predominant role in establishing this progressive view, not only because of its Hebrew foundation, but also because of its fundamental message concerning the Kingdom of God advancing in the earth. Prophets in the Old Testament spoke of a coming Kingdom that would endure forever and grow until it filled the earth (see 1 Chron. 17:12; Dan. 2:44). This was contrary to the thinking of all the ancient kingdoms, such as the Persian, Greek, or Roman, where people fatalistically believed that kingdoms rise and fall.

Jesus walked the streets of Israel declaring, *"The kingdom of God is at hand"*—which meant that the reign of God in the earth had begun. In several parables Jesus explained how the Kingdom of God is growing like seeds in the earth: first they sprout, then they develop roots, then they push upward, and finally they develop into mature plants (see Mark 4:2-8;26-29). In another parable He explained how the Kingdom is growing like yeast in dough, little by little, eventually permeating the whole lump of dough (see Matt. 13:33). Modern Christians understand these parables in different ways, but the historical Church primarily held to a view called amillennialism, which envisioned the Kingdom of God continually growing in the earth like seeds in soil or yeast in dough. They believed the Kingdom of God would grow as the Church grows until it fills the whole earth.[2]

During the 1800s, most Evangelical Christians believed that the Church would be successful in establishing the Kingdom of God on earth before the return of Jesus—a doctrine known as postmillennialism. One outworking of this belief was the establishment of many universities founded for the purpose of establishing the Kingdom of God in this world. I will discuss this idea of the advancing Kingdom more in Section II, Chapter 39. For now I can say that the idea of an advancing kingdom along with the ancient Hebrew understanding of linear, progressive time were the foundation for Western society's understanding that society is advancing.

With this understanding, optimism came to dominate Western society during the 1800s. People believed that human progress was inevitable and that a bright future lies ahead. That optimism was reinforced by tremendous advancements in science and technology. The Industrial Revolution (mid-1700s through the 1800s) brought an enormous increase in many kinds of goods. Agricultural societies changed into industrialized societies. Millions of people migrated from rural areas to the cities. Of course, there were many drawbacks to the industrialization, and common laborers suffered, but generally speaking, the standard of living rose continuously during that period. Indeed, the world did appear to be getting better and better.

Optimism was especially prevalent in North America. This was the land of opportunities to which millions immigrated to obtain a better life. Thomas Jefferson, the Enlightenment president, called America "an experiment" in what humankind may accomplish when free. The eyes of Europe were on North America to see if, indeed, the New World would soar to greatness or fail.

Optimism of the 19th Century

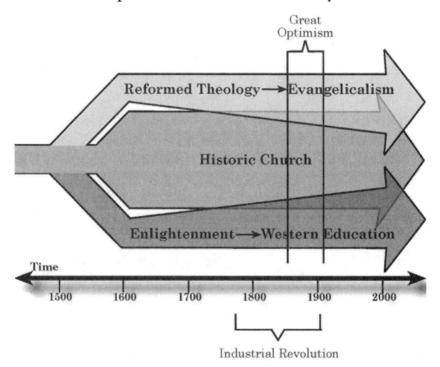

Discussion Questions

1. Consider and discuss Hegel's views that no one is ever totally right, but that progress is the result of violent struggles between competing forces. Do you think he was totally right?

2. What do you think of the world today? Are things getting better? Getting worse? In what ways?

Chapter 20

OPTIMISM FADES WITH THE GROWTH OF POSTMODERNISM

B Y THE END of the 19th century many people began to sense the emptiness and futility of living in a world that operates with the mathematical and mechanical precision proposed by Isaac Newton. Most people continued to hold to the idea that the world ran according to natural laws, however, they sought for another dimension to life.

As is true for most cultural transitions in society, the first people to express the need for change were those involved in the arts. They dreamed of more vital aspects of our being such as love, joy, passion, and sorrow. Composers, painters, writers, and other creative individuals aimed at the heart of people rather than the mind. The transition they fostered became known as *Romanticism*.

This period was accompanied by similar feelings and changes in religion. People drifted away from the cold and formal structure of Lutheranism and Calvinism. Revivals charged with emotion became popular, especially in America. Fiery preachers followed in the footsteps of John Wesley (1703-1791). The denomination he founded, Methodism, surged in growth to such an extent that it became the largest denomination in the United States by the time of the Civil War.

This movement was also important for the development of today's Evangelicals. As we discussed in Chapter 17, Reformed theology is the foundation of modern Evangelical Christianity, but the revivalists of the 19th century injected it with passion and zeal along with a definite message that each individual can and must make a personal commitment to Jesus Christ.

During the same period, the old, established mainline church denominations (i.e., Congregational, Presbyterian, and Episcopal), which had been the largest denominations in North America before 1800, declined in membership and influence. There are many things we can point to as the cause of this decline, but one of the most important factors was the work of liberal theologians who undermined the authority of the Scriptures, and hence, the authority of Christianity. In their well-researched book *The Churching of America, 1776-2005,* Roger Finke and Rodney Stark provide documentation showing a correlation between churches declining and their increasing requirements for their own leaders to be theologically trained in seminaries. In contrast, Methodist and Baptist churches flourished as their ministers zealously evangelized America in the 1800s with little to no formal religious training.

Even today, many church leaders of the mainline denominations talk begrudgingly about the secularization of Western society over the last 200 years. Yet, at the same time, modern church groups unhindered by years of formal academic religious training have flourished and continue to do so.

Although it is not as bad as the old mainline denominational leaders would have us believe, there has been a secularization throughout Western society. The Scientific Revolution followed by the Enlightenment provided the intelligentsia a worldview that needed no God. As this worldview was embraced by a large percentage of those in control of higher education, the stage was set for the shift. As is true of any time, whoever teaches the children, rules the future.

Another factor in the secularization of Western society was a reorientation of people's hearts, goals, and priorities toward the accumulation of material things. Capitalism produced great wealth and an accelerated rate of daily life. With a preoccupation with material things here and now, people no longer oriented their priorities toward the rewards or punishments awaiting them in the afterlife.

When Western civilization moved into the 20th century, attitudes concerning the future took a major shift. World War I (1914-1918) broke out, and people in Europe became disillusioned to the point of skepticism. North Americans followed suit during the Great Depression, followed by World War II (1935-1945). They had witnessed the wickedness of which society is capable. The Jewish holocaust added to this realization. Still, Americans continued to be a little more hopeful than Europeans. Hope flared as John F. Kennedy cast a new vision, but that was doused with his assassination; then defeat in Vietnam extinguished the remaining embers.

During the last half of the 20th century, people—Christians and non-Christians—became more pessimistic about the future of society, but they continued to have optimism for their personal lives. Americans still believed in the American dream and they were hopeful that their personal financial positions would get better and better. However, they lost hope that society as a whole would continue to progress. They lost confidence in governmental leadership. The news media and other forms of modern communication brought tragedies from all over the world into the living rooms of people's homes. The development of nuclear bombs and other weapons of mass destruction made everyone unsure of the future. This anxiety increased as these weapons were coming into the hands of hostile nations. Along with this came

AIDS, killing millions and making all aware of our vulnerability. At the same time, environmental concerns lunged to the forefront of conversations. Diminishing energy resources and global warming put tomorrow at risk.

Historians and philosophers like to think of our times as *Postmodern* and our thought patterns as those of *Postmodernity,* referring to that which displaced the thought patterns of the Modern Period.

Modernity Replaced by Postmodernity

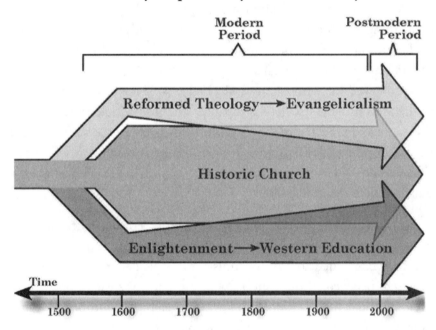

Hundreds of books have been written on Postmodernity, but it is too early to define what the thought patterns of the present culture are. Historians who live a century from now may see our times very differently than we do. One thing that is clear is that Enlightenment thought continues to lie at the heart of Postmodern thinking and of our Western educational systems. However, now people are skeptical of humanity's goodness. Rather than saying that people are inherently good or bad, a postmodern university student may say, "My friends are okay, but everyone else is screwed up." Giving such answers that do not really say if people are good or bad is common for young postmodern adults because they are content with not having everything figured out and put in boxes like earlier generations expected. They are even comfortable holding ideas that contradict each other.

Concerning society and the future, views vary widely, but typical postmodern people have abiding questions as to whether or not humanity will even survive.

In contrast, most Evangelicals cling to the idea that people are inherently evil and society is deteriorating morally, ethically, and spiritually. This negative view of society is closely tied to a theological shift concerning the Kingdom of God. As skepticism and negative views of the future flooded into Western Christianity, most Evangelical Christians changed their view from postmillennialism to premillennialism. Rather than believing that the Church would be successful in establishing the Kingdom of God on earth (postmillennialism), most accepted premillennialism—which portrays the world getting worse and worse until the day Jesus comes back to bring judgment and then set up the Kingdom of God on earth.

I am not trying to say whether premillennialism or postmillennialism is correct. I am simply stating the historical fact that the postmillennialism of the 19th century inspired Christians to aggressively build schools and universities with hopes of changing society in positive ways. In contrast, premillennialism hinders planning for the future and carries with it threats of impending judgments, including economic collapse, famines, wars, and evil government takeovers.

	View of Reformed Theology	View of the Enlightenment	View of Postmodernity
I. God	In Control	Not Involved, Unproveable, Unknowable	Not Involved, Unproveable, Unknowable
II. Humanity	Inherently Evil	Inherently Good	?
III. World	Corrupt in Its Fallen State	Wonderful in Its Natural State	Wonderful in Its Natural State
IV. Society	Deteriorating	Advancing	?

What is true? Who is right? We will answer these questions in Section II.

Discussion Questions

1. In preparation for Section II of our discussion, what do you think of the modern Evangelical worldview, which sees people as inherently evil and society as deteriorating morally, ethically, and spiritually?

2. Given the fluctuations of Western civilization's outlook on the world's conditions since the 1800s, how might you judge today's popular outlook of the world condition? Optimistic? Pessimistic? Realistic? Driven by similar or different forces than those from the past?

SUMMARY OF SECTION I

THROUGHOUT SECTION I, we followed the development of the
Western worldview with a focus on how Christian thought was laid
upon the foundation of the ancient Greek spiritual/natural division.
Western philosophy was particularly molded by that division and,
because it developed intertwined with theology, the historical Church
has been profoundly influenced. As a result, even today Christianity and
all Western thought remain profoundly influenced by the ancient Greek
spiritual/natural division.

Development of the Western Worldview

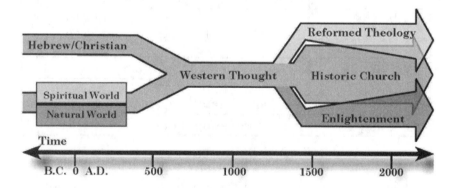

Western Christianity remains tied to Augustinian thought, with
Reformed theology clinging to the three points of Augustinian thought

concerning God, humanity, and the world. On those three topics, Enlightenment thought offers very different conclusions than Reformed theology. We have examined those conclusions, and we also saw where the Scientific Revolution led people to accept the ideas that God is unknowable and His existence cannot be proven.

We also saw how Reformed theology is the foundation for modern Evangelicalism while Enlightenment thought lies at the foundation of our modern Western education.

Finally, we considered periods in recent Western history of optimism and skepticism. Evangelicals and advocates of Reformed theology were optimistic during the 1800s, but throughout most of the 1900s they were pessimistic about the future of society. Enlightenment thinkers were positive during the 1800s and most of the 1900s, but their thoughts have recently been replaced by the skepticism of the postmodern mind.

	Reformed Theology Which is the Foundation for Evangelicalism	The Enlightenment Which is the Foundation for Western Education
I. God	In Control	Not Involved Unproveable Unknowable
II. Humanity	Inherently Evil	Inherently Good
III. World	Corrupt in Its Fallen State	Wonderful in Its Natural State
IV. Society	Deteriorating	Advancing

If we want to develop Christianity separate from the Western worldview, then we must go all the way back to the foundation and re-lay biblical truths upon the early Hebrew/Christian foundation. We must also separate Christianity from Western philosophy. Only then can we rethink all of the above issues and come up with Christianity separate from Western thought and culture. That is what we will do in Section II.

SECTION II

REBUILDING OUR CHRISTIANITY
APART FROM THE
WESTERN WORLDVIEW

Introduction to Section II

IT IS DIFFICULT FOR US WESTERNERS to fully grasp how deeply rooted the spiritual/natural division is within our own minds. Not only our thoughts but our vocabulary has been rooted in the ancient Greek worldview. It is most difficult for those of us who have been indoctrinated into studies of Western science, philosophy, and theology.[1] Christians who find the teachings of Augustine and Calvin agreeable to their own beliefs have an especially difficult time thinking independently of the foundation laid by Plato and Aristotle.[2]

To emphasize how deeply rooted the spiritual/natural division is, let's consider a we-have-always-done-it-that-way story. Historians tell us that the following often-quoted story is not entirely accurate; however, if we simply look at it as a story, it makes the point.

The standard distance between railroad tracks in the United States. is 4 feet, 8.5 inches. Why? Because that is the way they built them in England, and the English engineers were responsible for building the first railway systems in the United States. Why did the English build tracks spaced 4 feet, 8.5 inches apart? Because the people who built the rail lines in England were the same people who built the prerail tramways. Why did they use the 4 feet, 8.5 inches spacing? Because the people who built those tramways used the same jigs and tools that were used for spacing the distance between wheels in horse-drawn wagons.

Why were the wagon wheels spaced 4 feet, 8.5 inches apart? Because if they were spaced any other distance, some of the wagon wheels would break on the old roads of England where the ruts in the roads were 4 feet, 8.5 inches. So why were the ruts at that distance apart from each other? Imperial Rome built the first long distance roads in Europe for their legions, and their chariots had wheels that were 4 feet, 8.5 inches apart. And why were the wheels on their chariots 4 feet, 8.5 inches apart? Because that is the average distance between the rear ends of two horses standing side by side.

This illustration is meant to show how present human endeavors and thoughts can often be traced all the way back to ancient times. More importantly, it reveals how people have a difficult time breaking free of tracks that were laid down many years in the past.

The tracks laid down by the ancient Greeks are still firmly guiding (and limiting) Christianity. Therefore, we need to go all the way to the foundation and derail our own thoughts off of the spiritual/natural framework. Only if we set Christianity upon the ancient Hebrew foundation—which sees no wall between the spiritual and natural realms—will we have Christianity separated from Western thought.

As Christians, we value the foundation of the ancient Hebrew people because it was developed as they related to God. He worked among them as they came out of Egypt and were formed into a people with their own culture and land. God was communicating with and leading them. It was under His guidance that their laws and traditions were molded.

Today this foundation is more naturally understood by people groups who have not been indoctrinated into the Western educational system. Many of the tribal people with whom I have worked in Africa have a foundation with absolutely no wall between the spiritual and natural realms. Therefore, when they embrace Christianity, the spiritual and supernatural dimensions are very real to them. They have other problems associated with their own cultural backgrounds but, in at least this one area, they develop a form of Christianity more true to the biblical revelation than Christians in developed Western nations.

In the modern Church, Western intellectualism has played a significant role in choking the life out of vibrant Christianity. Many churches and denominations have experienced spiritual death after trying to become more sophisticated and intellectually respectable. Some regrettably talk about a "religious spirit," using this terminology in a negative sense to refer to Christianity that has morphed into lifeless form and meaningless ritual. Of course, there can be many different causes of spiritual deadness (such as broken relationships, unforgiveness, disobedience to God, lack of prayer, etc.). But there is no doubt that many Christian leaders have lost the energy that once invigorated their ministries as a result of pursuing intellectual excellence, which ultimately resulted in a form of godliness void of God's power.

On the other hand, there is a vibrancy that is undeniable in many Christian ministries that are led by leaders who have worked hard at tearing down the spiritual/natural barrier. One of my favorite teachers and authors is Bill Johnson, who pastors a large church in northern California. His worldview is identifiable in his best-selling book, *When Heaven Invades Earth*. Notice that even the title tears down the wall between the spiritual and natural realms. Pastor Johnson's church is named "Bethel," which means the "house of God," a name coined by Jacob to refer to the location where he saw a ladder upon which angels ascended and descended between Heaven and earth (see Gen. 28:12-17). Pastor Johnson's church is strongly oriented toward creating an environment in which people can experience God. In his church and many others with similar vitality, what is most evident is that the heart, not the intellect, brings spiritual phenomena into the natural realm.

To the observant, the lesson is clear: there are things that we can do to keep our churches, our loved ones, and ourselves spiritually alive. One essential is a worldview that has no barrier between the spiritual and the natural realms—a worldview that recognizes the nearness of God. That worldview I will develop in the following pages.

As I develop a Christian worldview separate from the spiritual/natural division, I will need to address the three foundational points of God, humanity, and the world, over which Reformed theology and Enlightenment thought disagree. I will also talk about the nature of society, in the sense of it advancing or deteriorating.

	View of Reformed Theology	View of the Enlightenment	Christianity Separate from W. Worldview
I. God	In Control	Not Involved, Unproveable, Unknowable	
II. Humanity	Inherently Evil	Inherently Good	
III. World	Corrupt in Its Fallen State	Wonderful in Its Natural State	
IV. Society	Deteriorating	Advancing	

In developing this worldview, I will occasionally use the Bible. I am convinced that the Bible writers were inspired by God when they wrote the book. However, I am not giving a lot of attention to arguing this point because whether or not the Bible is inspired is not fully relevant for the following discussion. I will use the Bible to identify the world-view of the Bible writers in the same way that I would read the writings of any culture to determine their worldview. I will not be using the Bible to say this is right or that is wrong. I will simply identify how the Bible writers thought. What would Christianity be like if it were understood without the spiritual/natural division?

Introduction to Section II

I am not trying to convince the atheist or even the skeptic. I am trying to show the reasonableness of Christianity and at the same time offer a well-thought-out Christian worldview. The atheist is welcome to listen in order to learn how we think, but my primary aim is to offer to Christians a foundation for their faith, which will help them in all areas of their lives.

As discussed in Section I, Chapter 2, a foundation is something upon which a structure is built. If a building is being constructed, its shape and size are very much determined by the foundation upon which it is erected. There may be some variations in construction materials and designs, but the fundamental structure will be predetermined by the foundation undergirding the whole building. Let's lay our foundation now.

Chapter 21

GOD EXISTS AND HIS EXISTENCE IS OBVIOUS

THE ANCIENT HEBREW WORLDVIEW recognized one world with two realms: the spiritual realm and natural realm. They saw no wall between the spiritual and the natural realms. This is the foundational thought pattern of those who wrote the Bible. True Christianity is laid on this foundation.

The Bible uses vocabulary that corresponds to this foundation. Nowhere does it talk about the natural versus the supernatural. Nowhere does it speak in terms of here versus there.

Notice that I am not referring to Heaven when I speak of the spiritual dimension. Biblical thought does locate Heaven in a different location, but I am speaking of the invisible realm that is here and totally integrated with the visible universe.

Make no mistake, this is the foundation of biblical thought. The Bible opens with God creating the universe, that is, the invisible God preparing a natural realm in which people can live, eat, and work. Then we see God walking and talking with Adam. He is not far away; God is very interested in what is happening in this world. He watches over and communicates intimately with Enoch, Noah, Abraham, and Moses. The Hebrew people become His people, and He is their God. He leads them in the wilderness in a cloud by day and a pillar of fire by night. God gives them the Promised Land, a gift that is natural, real, and relative to their daily needs. God speaks with His people through prophets and leads their judges and kings.

In the New Testament we see God incarnate as the Word became flesh. He walked among people teaching and healing them. After Jesus ascended into Heaven, God sent His Spirit to dwell within His people. They became His temple; He became their comforter and counselor. God covenants with His people to give them a new heart and to lead them by His Spirit, causing them to walk in His ways. This is not a distant God, but as Paul wrote, *"He is not far from each one of us"* (Acts 17:27).

I am not pointing these things out expecting the unbeliever to accept them as true. I am merely identifying the foundational worldview of those who wrote the Bible. Rather than see the spiritual realm as separate and distant, they saw the spiritual and natural realms as inseparable. In fact, they did not even see the spiritual realm as above while the natural realm is down here below. The biblical worldview identifies the spiritual realm as here—simply another dimension filling the same location as the natural dimension.

To emphasize this, I will draw my diagrams showing the spiritual and natural realms side by side, rather than one above the other. Realize that even that does not adequately reveal how the spiritual and natural realms are fully integrated. They actually should be seen as overlapping each other, filling the same space.

The Biblical and Ancient Hebrew Foundation

With this understanding we will see no wall between the spiritual and natural realms. A good comparison of God moving from the spiritual realm into the natural is a person stepping out of the shadows and into the light. There is no wall, just a simple step from one realm into the other.

If we have this as the foundation of our worldview, then God's existence is obvious. If we rid our minds of the imaginary wall erected by Western intellectualism, then God's existence is *"clearly seen"* and all of humanity is *"without excuse"* (Rom. 1:20). I explained this in Section I, Chapter 11, and I will not repeat that discussion other than to say that proof for the existence of a Stuff Creator is the existence of stuff. It is irrational to conclude that nothing is responsible for something. It is absurd to intellectually deny God's existence.

This truth is hidden from those whose thought patterns are fixed in the ruts laid down by the ancient Greek philosophers and deepened by Western philosophical thought. Further blinding them is Western intellectualism, which places God in the spiritual, unknowable world. Yet, just because *they* are blind is no reason for Christians to be blind. Just because *they* cannot see is no reason for Christians to likewise say that God's existence is unprovable.

	View of Reformed Theology	View of the Enlightenment	Christianity Separate from W. Worldview
I. God	In Control	Not Involved, Unproveable, Unknowable	Exists, Existence Obvious
II. Humanity	Inherently Evil	Inherently Good	
III. World	Corrupt in Its Fallen State	Wonderful in Its Natural State	
IV. Society	Deteriorating	Advancing	

Of course, a Christian with eyes to see may talk to the unbeliever and even use their vocabulary in discussing the existence of God. However, the Christian need not embrace their worldview. For their own worldview, Christians should confidently lay biblical truths on the ancient Hebrew foundation. Hence, to us, God's existence is obvious.

Now as we go on to develop our worldview, this will be our starting point: God exists and His existence is obvious. This is Christianity separate from the Western worldview.[1]

Discussion Questions

1. What difference does it make in one's Christian life whether the spiritual and natural worlds are understood as separated or integrated? How important is this distinction?

2. Is the atheist's position—that God does not exist—absurd?

Chapter 22

GOD IS ALIVE AND HE IS GOOD

T HE APOSTLE PAUL revealed truths about the nature of God as he reasoned with the Greek philosophers, saying:

Being then the children of God, we ought not to think that the Divine Nature is like gold or silver or stone, an image formed by the art and thought of man (Acts 17:29).

Paul was making the argument that we are "living," and therefore, whoever or whatever is responsible for our existence must have life Himself.[1] He is not like a statue, but rather He must be "living."

Note that I am not using Scripture to prove that God is living. Instead, I am using Paul's argument because it is a reasonable argument. Philosophers have used similar arguments throughout history. They point out that the cause must be greater than the effect. Since God created us with life, He must have life or something greater than life within Himself.

On another occasion, Paul declared:

...a living God, who made the heaven and the earth and the sea and all that is in them. In the generations gone by He permitted all the nations to go their own ways; and yet He did not leave Himself without witness, in that He did good and gave you rains

from heaven and fruitful seasons, satisfying your hearts with food and gladness (Acts 14:15-17).

Paul was talking about people *"in generations gone by,"* people who had never heard the Gospel, who had never heard about Jesus. We are told that even they had a witness concerning God. What was that witness? There are three parts:

1. He did good;

2. He gave them rains;

3. He gave them fruitful seasons.

These things satisfied their hearts with food and gladness. Paul was implying that every person on earth, even if they live in a primitive village never exposed to modern society, has enough information to know that there is a God and that He is good.

Of course, the atheist could easily argue against this, and I would agree that rains and fruitful seasons are not proof that God is good. We know, in fact, that many places on earth do not have enough rain and the seasons are not always fruitful. Therefore, the next two chapters will deal with the age-old question, "If God is good, why is there so much suffering in the world?"

For now we can note Paul's argument that the rains and fruitful seasons are "witnesses" of God's goodness. They are not proof of His goodness, but they are evidence of it. Of course, people may reject or accept this evidence. Or they simply may want more evidence before they decide.

At this point we can compare God's relationship with humanity to a man's relationship with a wild dog. That dog may be too timid to approach, but the man may leave food in places where the wild animal will find it, hoping that one day the wild dog will trust him and allow him to be a friend. Similarly, the Stuff Creator did not create a huge torture machine, but He put us in a world where humanity has what it needs to live and be happy.

Again, I will say that people can reasonably reject this witness of God's goodness. I am not presenting this as proof of God's goodness. Instead, I am explaining how Christians think. We see the Stuff Creator as good, and therefore, we accept that which is good in the world as coming from God.

	View of Reformed Theology	View of the Enlightenment	Christianity Separate from W. Worldview
I. God	In Control	Not Involved, Unproveable, Unknowable	Exists, Existence Obvious, Living, Good
II. Humanity	Inherently Evil	Inherently Good	
III. World	Corrupt in Its Fallen State	Wonderful in Its Natural State	
IV. Society	Deteriorating	Advancing	

To hold to the idea that God is good with any sense of integrity, we must explain why there is so much bad in the world and from where it comes. Let's give this topic our attention in the next two chapters.

Discussion Questions

1. What are some of the popular arguments for holding that God is either all good or all bad? Is there equal evidence for both?

2. What is your personal view (on question 1), and what shaped that view?

Chapter 23

GOD'S INVOLVEMENT IN THIS WORLD

ONCE WE have accepted the truth of God's existence, then we can discuss God's ongoing involvement with this world. Reformed theology teaches that God is in complete control of all things (Augustine, Luther, and Calvin would agree). The view of the Enlightenment is that God is not involved in this world. Who is right?

Let's study this by examining the Bible through the context in which it was written, which is the ancient Hebrew worldview. At this point we do not need to *prove* how God is involved in this world. Let's simply see what the Bible writers thought on this subject. Once we have determined their worldview in this respect, then we can see how that view matches the view of Reformed theology and/or the view of the Enlightenment. We will also be able to see what answers that view offers concerning the presence of evil and suffering in the world.

The Bible identifies five different levels of God's interaction with this world:

1.   God's sovereign interventions

2.   God's answers to prayer

3.   God's relationships with people

4. God's anointings on people

5. God's spiritual laws

I will briefly discuss each of these.

1. Sovereign Interventions

A biblical worldview leads us to understand that God is sovereign in the sense that He can intervene in the affairs of this world at any time He chooses. The Bible is filled with testimonies of His interventions, especially in the lives of the Jews.

2. Answers to Prayer

God does, at times, answer prayer.

3. Relationships With People

God influences this world through His relationships with individuals. As people relate to Him, they bring their lives more into alignment with His will. This can be compared to relationships people have with one another. For example, when a young man falls in love with a woman, his behavior typically changes, often in dramatic ways. He will desire to engage in activities that please her and cease doing things that would harm their relationship. Similarly, when a person enters into a relationship with God, his or her life is brought more into alignment with God's will.

4. Anointings on People

God influences this world through the anointings He puts on individual's lives. To see this, think of God's anointing as a deposit of the Holy Spirit that empowers an individual to accomplish some task in this world. For example, we are told in Deuteronomy 31:3-6 that craftsmen were anointed by God to do their work with extra skill and wisdom. Through such anointings, God does not *control* the individual because the anointed person has the authority to use or not use the anointing. In the Bible we see reports of people who had an activation of God's Spirit enabling them to prophesy. However, they maintained the authority to use or not use that gift. The apostle Paul explained how the spirits of prophets are subject to the prophets (see 1 Cor. 14:32). This principle also applies to other areas of life in which God empowers individuals with His Spirit.

5. Spiritual Laws

The fifth means by which we see God influencing this world is through the establishment of spiritual laws. As I use the term *spiritual,* do not think with the Western worldview that restricts a spiritual law to its influence in the spiritual dimension. The spiritual and natural realms are integrated; things in one realm influence things in the other realm. In this context, I am referring to how certain human behaviors cause specific changes due to spiritual laws that God has instilled within Creation.

For an example, consider what the apostle Paul tells us in Galatians 6:7: *"...whatever a man sows, this he will also reap."* If we accept this as a spiritual law, then we will recognize a cause-and-effect relationship between people's actions and the consequences of their actions. This is not the result of God's direct intervention or His control of each person's life. Rather, the principle of sowing and reaping is the result of God instilling this spiritual law within Creation from the beginning. It is simply how things work.

For another example, consider Paul's exhortation:

Honor your father and mother...so that it may be well with you, and that you may live long on the earth (Ephesians 6:2-3).

If we accept this as truth, then we will see a cause-and-effect relationship between honoring one's parents and having a good, long life. It is not that God reacts to each person's behavior toward his or her parents, and hence, intervenes in the affairs of each person's life making things good or bad. Rather God instilled within Creation itself the principle that honoring one's parents releases blessings into one's life.

Finally, consider the law of giving. In several Bible passages we are taught that if we give to God's work and to the poor, we will be blessed (see 2 Cor. 9:6-11, for example). Of course, God could sovereignly respond each time a person gives, but the law of giving and receiving that God instilled within Creation may work without His direct intervention.

If we accept such spiritual laws along with the other four levels of God's interactions, then we will develop a biblical view of God's interactions with this world. These five levels are evident in the ancient Hebrew worldview. An observant Bible student may be able to identify other forms of interaction, but these are the most obvious. This was the worldview of Abraham, Isaac, and Jacob.

God's Interaction With This World

| Sovereign Interventions | Answers to Prayer | Relationships | Anointings | Spiritual Laws |

It is also worth noting that God is working out His plans in the earth. In particular, we are told that He is working all things out with a view to the summing up of all things in Christ (see Eph. 1:9-10). Through His interactions with humanity and through His sovereign interventions in the affairs of this world, God is orchestrating things so that His ultimate will is being carried out.

In the next chapter we will see how this meshes with the views of Reformed theology and/or the Enlightenment. We also will see the importance of incorporating this understanding into our Christian worldview, and in particular, our understanding of evil and suffering in the world.

Discussion Questions

1. As seen through the biblical worldview, is God's interaction with humanity primarily restricted to the spiritual realm?

2. In light of our present discussion on the integration of the natural and spiritual worlds, how should we view the idea (which some Christians hold) that the spiritual world must be impacted first before we will experience change in the natural world?

Chapter 24

GOD IS SELECTIVELY
INVOLVED IN THIS WORLD

IN THE LAST CHAPTER we identified the biblical worldview, which includes at least five ways in which God influences this world:

1. God's sovereign interventions

2. God's answers to prayer

3. God's relationships with people

4. God's anointings on people

5. God's spiritual laws

If we embrace these five, then we must reject the views of both Enlightenment thought and Reformed theology. Let me explain.

The Enlightened thinker claims that God is not involved in any fashion with this world, while the biblical view shows God involved in at least five ways.

Christians holding to the views of Reformed theology claim that God is in control of all things, which also contradicts the biblical view. To see this, note first that God does intervene in this world. *If God was in control, then He would not have to intervene.*

In the last chapter, we noted that God is orchestrating the affairs of this world to fulfill His ultimate goals. However, His overriding hand of guidance does not mean that He is controlling every big and little thing. The biblical worldview leads us to believe that God is *selectively* involved in this world.

It is correct to say, "God is in control," if by this statement we are implying that nothing lies beyond the limits of God's ability to intervene. God can control anything He wants to because He has all authority and power to do whatever He wants to do. However, it is wrong to say, "God is in control," if by this statement we are implying that God is controlling everything in the world. In that sense, God is not in control.

To communicate this without confusion, let me say, "God is in charge."

Accepting this understanding, we can also recognize that this world functions according to natural laws set up by God at Creation. We can study those laws so as to predict future events. The leaders of the Scientific Revolution were correct on this point. However, Christians also understand that God can intervene—which is what we refer to as a miracle. Miracles are the exception to how the world normally runs. The world normally runs according to natural laws.

Furthermore, people have a free will. God can force them to do His will if He desires to, but He has chosen not to completely control everyone.

Contrary to Augustinian and Reformed thinking, I dare say that *God is not in control.* That is the very reason we pray, *"Thy kingdom come,*

Thy will be done on earth as it is in heaven...." We are taught to pray for God's will to be done here on earth because right now His will is not being totally done. There are things occurring that grieve His heart. There are human beings not doing His will. That is the problem with this world! A day will come when every knee bows and every tongue confesses Jesus Christ as Lord. Then God will fill all and be in all (see 1 Cor. 15:25-28). Then all beings will be in submission to God, and His will shall be done throughout all of Creation.

But at the present time, God's will is not being totally carried out in the world. This view is important for several reasons, four of which I will mention here.

First, the biblical view of God's involvement in the world (as identified here) does not line up with what Reformed Christianity teaches. As a consequence, we do not have to offer to non-Christians the God proposed by Reformed theology. There is a middle ground between complete control and no control. As I stated, *God is selectively involved in this world.*

The second reason this is important is because it allows scientific advancement. Many atheists see Christianity as the enemy of science. In reality, what undermines scientific advancement is not Christianity, but the false idea that many Christians have that spiritual beings—whether they be God, angels, or demons—are controlling everything. Anyone who believes spiritual beings are controlling everything cannot study the natural laws that govern this world with any sense of earnestness and expectation of success.

The third reason this is important is because it places responsibility for the care of this world where it belongs—on us. If we say that God is controlling everything, then we go back to the victimization of the Middle Ages. Let's not do that.

The fourth reason it is important to recognize God's selective involvement with this world is because it answers the question of the ages: "If God is in control, why is there so much suffering in this world?" This question has been repeated millions of times by inquiring minds. Closely related is the single most frequently raised objection to the existence of God: "I cannot believe in God because there is so much suffering in the world."

A person who makes these statements has only two options in mind: either God is in control or He is completely uninvolved. Because they cannot accept the first option, they choose the second—which is not a bad choice if we consider the implications. If God is in control, then He is responsible for all of the pain and suffering in the world. If God is in control, then He is the one killing babies, causing war, and spreading diseases. There is no way around this: if God is in complete control, then He is responsible for everything. If I had to choose between that God and no God, I would be hard pressed for a decision on which to base my life.

Hallelujah! There is a third option—a biblical worldview. The world is running according to natural laws, and people have a free will. God may sovereignly intervene, and He does influence this world through responses to prayer, relationships, anointings, and spiritual laws. A day will come when all things will be in submission to God and then *"there will no longer be any mourning, or crying, or pain...."* (Rev. 21:3-4). However, at the present time, the reason there is so much suffering in this world is because God is not in control.

Natural disasters happen because this world is running according to natural laws. People hurt one another because they have a free will. Although I will not be discussing this further, a biblical worldview also leads us to believe that there is evil in this world in the form of evil spiritual beings. These are the sources of pain and suffering.[1]

	View of Reformed Theology	View of the Enlightenment	Christianity Separate from W. Worldview
I. God	In Control	Not Involved, Unproveable, Unknowable	Exists, Existence Obvious, Living, Good, Selectively Involved
II. Humanity	Inherently Evil	Inherently Good	
III. World	Corrupt in Its Fallen State	Wonderful in Its Natural State	
IV. Society	Deteriorating	Advancing	

This idea of God not being in control can be shocking and challenging when first heard by Christians raised in Reformed theology and in some other branches of Evangelical Christianity. It is, however, the worldview of Abraham, Isaac, and Jacob. It is also the conclusion we would come to if we separate Christianity from the Western worldview.

Discussion Questions

1. To what extent do you think God is in control of this world? To what level of detail do you think He controls it?

2. If you agree with the discussion that says God applies selective control in this world, then what do you think affects God's level of involvement?

Chapter 25

KNOWING THE TRUTH ABOUT JESUS

W E HAVE DISCUSSED God and His involvement in this world, but as Christians we cannot stop there. We must go on to offer a sound basis for our belief in Jesus Christ.

According to the apostle Paul, the resurrection is proof that Jesus Christ is the One sent by God:

> ...God is now declaring to men that all people everywhere should repent, because He has fixed a day in which He will judge the world in righteousness through a Man whom He has appointed, having furnished proof to all men by raising Him from the dead (Acts 17:30-31).

God has *"furnished proof."* Of course, the non-Christian is not going to easily accept the validity of the resurrection. The rationalist's worldview doesn't even allow for the possibility of such a miracle. Yet the Christian must not back down from the resurrection being the primary proof of Christianity. There are other reasons to believe, but the resurrection is the "proof" that God has given to humanity.

In saying this, I am not implying that it is our responsibility to convince the non-Christian that Jesus rose from the grave. That is impossible. As I explained in Chapter 11, we cannot prove to anyone that

171

bacteria exist if they are unwilling to look through a microscope. Nor can we prove to non-Christians that Jesus rose from the grave if they refuse to accept the possibility that miracles can happen.

Therefore, we need to focus upon our own discovery and validation of truth. And indeed, I say again that a Christian should use his or her mind in every way possible to determine what truth is. However, our worldview does not need to exclude miracles. It is totally rational to believe in miracles if, indeed, there is a God. All we need for miracles to happen is a miracle-working God—One who is powerful and creative—One who can intervene in the affairs of this world.

Notice that our worldview is broader than the worldview of the rationalist. We are more open-minded, believing both in science and in the possibility of miracles.

With our broader worldview, let's consider the possibility that Jesus did rise from the dead. On what basis do we know this to be true? First and foremost, we have the testimony of those who lived in the first century and saw Jesus alive after He was crucified.

Of course, the non-Christian may not accept the testimony of those first-century men and women. In fact, the rationalist claims that he or she only accepts as fact that which can be observed and tested. Yet if we analyze this claim of the rationalist, we find that it is pure foolishness. To analyze this claim, we must take a short diversion from our investigation of the resurrection of Jesus. It is important to first discuss the means by which we access truth.

Consider the fact that most, if not all, rationalists have accepted the idea that Julius Caesar was a leader of the Roman Empire during the first century B.C. Why does the rationalist believe this? No modern-day rationalist was alive to see Caesar. Very few modern individuals have been involved firsthand with archaeology or the study of ancient writings from that period. In reality, most people today know about Julius Caesar because of what they have read or been told by others.

Next consider this: every rationalist has accepted the fact that Antarctica is a continent located to the south. How does the rationalist know this to be true? I doubt that even one in a hundred rationalists have ever observed Antarctica for themselves. They accept its existence simply because they have been taught that it exists.

How does the rationalist know that right now there are automobiles in Liberia, Africa? Perhaps they saw them on television or someone has described what they observed while visiting that country. But very few rationalists in the Western world have observed those cars for themselves.

How does one know that the world events reported on the news are really true? Of course, we cannot know with 100-percent certainty, but even rationalists accept most of what is reported without personally observing those reported events.

I could offer thousands of examples, but the point is clear: most of what people accept as fact has never been observed and tested by themselves. The vast majority of all that we know has come to us through what other people have communicated to us.

Furthermore, we accept many things without question, that is, without testing. For example, let the rationalist think about what he will be served for dinner this evening. How does he know that his food is not poisonous? He does not take the time to observe and test to see that it is safe to eat that meal. Is he taking a blind leap of faith by eating what is set before him? Not really, because he has some level of trust in the people who prepare the food. That is not blind faith because experience leads one to believe that certain people can be trusted to prepare food safely.

The liberal professor will rarely admit this because he or she wants to hold and promote the myth that all he or she has accepted as truth has been observed and tested. At the same time the liberal professor may state or imply that what one has learned through religious instruction or through one's parents has not been learned through the scientific method. Such a dichotomy between what the liberal professor holds as truth and what Christian parents and religious leaders hold as truth is pure fiction.

All people know what they know primarily through what has been communicated to them. Furthermore, the truths held by our forefathers and religious leaders have been no less observed and tested than most of what the liberal professor holds to be true.

Take, for example, the moral value held by Christian parents and religious leaders that sexual promiscuity is destructive to one's life. The liberal professor may state or imply that such values are just religious restrictions placed upon people without any observation and testing to establish such values. In reality, when parents tell their children to avoid sexual promiscuity, they are not speaking from a groundless belief system. Rather they have the wisdom of the ages, reinforced by the observations of many generations. They also have their own observations that formed during their growing years of watching their friends and others experience the consequences of sexual promiscuity.

Of course, there are some beliefs held by our forefathers that should no longer be embraced. Indeed, if we have observed and tested truth that contradicts a previously held idea, then we should discard the old ideas. However, there are also values and ethical issues that have been tested over the course of hundreds of years, and therefore, they should be accepted as the most verifiable truths presently available to humanity.

Our focus here is to show how truth is accessed by individuals. All people believe what they believe primarily through what they have been taught rather than through what they have personally observed and tested.

The idea that modern Enlightened ideas have been scientifically verified while Christian values have not been observed and tested is foolish.

Realizing that most of what we know comes through the testimony of others, let's take the next chapter to examine the testimony concerning the resurrection of Jesus Christ from the dead.

Discussion Questions

1. In general, how can we be sure of what we know about anything?

2. How much of what we accept as truth is obtained by firsthand observation and how much is by accepting the report of others?

3. How does our standard of what we will accept as truth vary between things we want to believe versus things we do not want to believe?

Chapter 26

EVIDENCE FOR THE RESURRECTION

W HEN WE consider the truth of Jesus' resurrection from the dead, the issue is not whether we can observe and test it for ourselves. The real issue has to do with whether or not we accept the testimony of those who say they witnessed the death and then saw the resurrected Lord.

Of course, the acceptance of the resurrection would demand a change in one's life. In contrast, if a person accepts the idea that Julius Caesar was once the leader of the Roman Empire, little is at risk. If a person admits that Jesus rose from the dead, then one's entire life is called into account. We must consider this because people have a tendency to believe what they want to believe. They also have a tendency to deny what they want to deny.[1]

If a person was to approach this issue with an unbiased mind—with a complete willingness to deal with the implications no matter what they might be—then what would they conclude about the testimony of those first-century witnesses?

To answer this, we first need to consider the written records from that time period. It is not only the Bible that records the events of the resurrection. For example, we have the writings of Josephus who was a

Jewish historian hired by the Roman government to write the history of the Jewish people. He wrote:

> Now, there was about this time Jesus, a wise man, if it be lawful to call him a man, for he was a doer of wonderful works— a teacher of such men as receive the truth with pleasure. He drew over to him both many of the Jews, and many of the Gentiles. He was [the] Christ; and when Pilate, at the suggestion of the principal men amongst us, had condemned him to the cross, those that loved him at the first did not forsake him, for he appeared to them alive again the third day. As the divine prophets had foretold these and ten thousand other wonderful things concerning him; and the tribe of Christians, so named from him, are not extinct at this day.[2]

Josephus was not a Christian, but he was a Jewish historian living during the first century. Yet, Josephus recognized how Jesus fulfilled the words of the prophets written many years earlier. For example, King David had written prophetically hundreds of years earlier that the Messiah could not be held in the grave (see Ps. 16:10; Acts 2:27). So then, we have prophetic words written before the resurrection and we have eyewitness accounts written after the resurrection.

Other non-Christian historians of the period who wrote about Jesus (but not His resurrection), include Tacitus,[3] Pliny the Younger,[4] Suetonius,[5] and Lucian.[6]

When we talk about eyewitness accounts recorded in the New Testament, skeptics too often dismiss them because they are recorded in one book—the Bible. Since they do not accept the Bible, they tend to dismiss its testimony of the resurrection. In reality, the Bible is a compilation of many writings from many authors. Matthew, Mark, Luke,[7] and John, who were eyewitnesses of the death and resurrection of Jesus, each wrote their own accounts of the events. During the first century, those writings about the life of Jesus were not compiled in one book, but they were circulated around the early Church in letters. Therefore, when the skeptics dismiss the Bible, they are dismissing several writings and several authors.

Luke, who was a physician, wrote that Jesus appeared many times over the course of 40 days (see Acts 1:3). The apostle Paul noted that Jesus had appeared to more than 500 people at one time (see 1 Cor. 15:6).

We should note that the apostles did not blindly accept as truth the resurrection of Jesus. When Mary Magdalene first saw the resurrected Lord, she went and told the apostles, but they did not believe her (see Mark 16:9-11; Luke 24:10-11). When Jesus appeared to the apostles, He showed them the wounds in His hands and feet (see Luke 24:40). Thomas refused to believe until he put his finger into those wounds (see John 20:24-27). Dr. Luke wrote that Jesus gave them many convincing proofs (see Acts 1:3).

Notice that these are the very actions that are considered today as the scientific method: observing and testing. In reality, the scientific method was not discovered in the 16th or 17th centuries. People have always used observation and testing to determine truth.

Those apostles verified for themselves the truth of the resurrection to such an extent that they were willing to base the rest of their lives on it. This is obvious by the historical records—in the Bible and in extra-biblical writings—which tell us that each and every one of the original apostles (except Judas) suffered persecution, torture, and/or martyrdom, unwilling to deny the resurrection.

For example, Doubting Thomas who once was the greatest skeptic, gave his life as a missionary to the East, even as far as India. Today we still have numerous writings dated from the first through fourth centuries describing his work in that region. There are also ancient church structures and many artifacts giving evidence of his presence and his works there. In the end, he died as a martyr, being persecuted intensely and finally being speared in A.D. 72. Such commitment until death by Thomas and the other apostles reveals how sure each of those men were concerning what they themselves witnessed.

For us to consider the validity of those first-century witnesses is not some strange practice nor exception to how we normally obtain truth. It is, in reality, the way we access most of the truths we embrace concerning everything we know. Therefore, it is only reasonable to ask ourselves if there is any more solid testimony than one that is held in the presence of torture and martyrdom (all except Judas and John were martyred).

It is worth noting that the first apostles did not stay in a tight-knit community where they could hold each other accountable to say the same story. Today we have hundreds of ancient writings that speak about their travels and missionary endeavors. As individuals they gave their lives and stood in the face of torture and martyrdom.

If a modern judge and jury consisted of people who held a worldview that allowed for the possibilities of miracles, then the testimonies of the first-century witnesses would easily stand up in a court of law today. Again, we can note that there is no more sure testimony than that which is maintained in the face of torture.

What we decide about the credibility of those witnesses is the single most important conclusion we can make in this life. As the apostle Paul declared:

> ...God is now declaring to men that all people everywhere should repent, because He has fixed a day in which He will judge the world in righteousness through a Man whom He has appointed,

having furnished proof to all men by raising Him from the dead (Acts 17:30-31).

If, indeed, Jesus rose from the dead, then a miracle has happened. If, indeed, Jesus rose from the dead, then God has intervened in history. Hence, we have proof that God sent Jesus and that God is alive!

	View of Reformed Theology	View of the Enlightenment	Christianity Separate from W. Worldview
I. God	In Control	Not Involved, Unproveable, Unknowable	Exists, Existence Obvious, Living, Good, Selectively Involved, Sent/Raised Jesus
II. Humanity	Inherently Evil	Inherently Good	
III. World	Corrupt in Its Fallen State	Wonderful in Its Natural State	
IV. Society	Deteriorating	Advancing	

If Jesus rose from the dead, we also have hope that life after death is possible. We can even hope that we may experience another life.

However, we need to pay attention to the warning in the verse we just quoted:

...He [God] *has fixed a day in which He will judge the world in righteousness through a Man* [Jesus] *whom He has appointed....*(Acts 17:31)

If Jesus rose from the dead, we have strong reason to believe that one day we shall all stand before Him and give an account for what we have done during our lives.

If Jesus is going to execute judgment someday, then we have a basis for discerning right and wrong. Since He will judge, He determines what is right and wrong. Contrary to what the Enlightenment professor would have us believe, there is a standard for ethics.

Through reason, I have determined these things to be true:

1. God sent Jesus;

2. Jesus rose from the dead;

3. God has worked a miracle, and therefore, we have proof that God is alive;

4. Life after death is possible;

5. There will be a future judgment.

Because these things are true, I have believed and invested my life in them.

Discussion Questions

1. How does the acceptance of a truth change a person? Does it have to be absolutely true to effect personal change?

2. Is it possible to accept a truth and not be changed by it?

Chapter 27

ONE'S OWN EXPERIENCE WITH GOD

THE RESURRECTION OF JESUS is proof, but it is not the only proof
that God sent Jesus. There have been hundreds of scholarly books
written on this subject, and I do not have the space to repeat those discussions. However, I will include this one chapter to discuss the proof
that resides with the individual.

Consider Paul's testimony that one day he was traveling around
persecuting and even murdering Christians. Then Jesus spoke to him in
a blinding light (see Acts 22:6-8). Paul was so convinced that it was
indeed Jesus speaking to him that he risked all, changed the course of
his life, and eventually proved himself willing to be imprisoned and tortured for what he believed. Paul may have never seen Jesus while He was
walking the earth, nor was he a witness of the resurrection, but he had
a personal experience—which to him was proof.

Millions of people throughout history have testified to having a
personal experience with God. By saying "millions" I am not exaggerat-
ing. With over 2 billion people today claiming to be Christians and
many more millions throughout the last 2,000 years, it is very conservative to say that millions of Christians would testify to having had some
experience with God.

The atheist may reject the testimony of people's experience, but it is difficult to take away an individual's experience. As the blind man who was healed by Jesus said, *"...I was blind, now I see"* (John 9:25). In the face of confrontation by the religious leaders of his day, the previously blind man stood his ground declaring what he knew to be true. Intimidation and reasoned arguments could not take away his own experience.

Millions of people today will tell those who are willing to listen how God met them on some occasion. Multitudes will report answers to prayers and miracles they have seen.

In reality, it is impossible for any outsider to know what a specific individual has personally experienced. This puts the atheist in a very precarious position. With millions of people presently bearing witness to experiences that they have had with God, atheists and agnostics must deny all of their experiences. In the face of those witnesses, atheists and agnostics must maintain that every one of those millions of people are delusional or liars. Atheists must believe this even though they cannot prove that all of those people are delusional or liars. Since they cannot prove it, they are taking a blind leap to believe it. Indeed, the atheists are the ones putting blind faith in something for which they have no proof.

What if it is true? What if even one of the millions of people who say they have encountered God or have observed a miracle is telling the truth? If even one miracle has ever happened, then the atheist is up the creek without a paddle—and the creek is rushing toward a waterfall.

Finally, do I dare say it? Yes, I have experienced God. I have proof. Maybe I cannot convince you, but I was blind, and now I see.

Discussion Questions

1. Assuming you are a Christian, what led you to a belief in the resurrection of Jesus Christ?

2. Can you say that you have experienced God? If so, in what ways?

Chapter 28

CREATED IN THE IMAGE
OF GOD WITH SPIRITUAL SENSES

NOW WE turn our attention away from the nature and existence of God to discuss the nature of humanity. The first thing the Bible tells us about humanity is that God created us and we are created in His image:

> *God created man in His own image, in the image of God He created him* (Genesis 1:27).

There are many implications of this, but one of the most obvious is that people are different from animals. In some way, we are formed, patterned after, made in the likeness of God.[1]

The apostle Paul also held that every person has an inner awareness of God. In the context of explaining that all creation is declaring the existence and attributes of God, Paul wrote:

> *...that which is known about God is evident within them; for God made it evident to them* (Romans 1:19).

According to this verse, every person has an inner awareness of God.

This concept can be very challenging to people with a Western worldview because they tend to think that all knowledge is derived from reason or from information received through the physical senses. The apostle Paul wrote that there is some knowledge that has been *made evident by God*. It is instilled by God within people. Can this be true? Does a baby come into this world with an instilled awareness of God?

Information programmed into the genetic code is common to the animal kingdom. For example, birds taken from the nest and raised isolated from other birds will grow up knowing how to build a nest. A dog raised away from other dogs will act in many ways as its parents.

Even at birth human babies demonstrate certain awarenesses. For example, a baby knows to orient itself for help. It cries. It looks for a mother or a father. This being true, isn't it also possible that a human being knows to orient himself or herself toward God?

Whether information about God's existence is programmed into the genetic code or exists within some invisible portion of a person, we do have evidence that some God-awareness is innate within people. Evidence of this God-awareness is the fact that every culture has developed practices to appease invisible beings greater than themselves. With over 6 billion people in the world today, over 2 billion claim to be Christian and 1.4 billion claim to be Muslim. Add to those numbers the tens of millions who believe in God but do not align themselves with Christianity or Islam. Then we have several hundred million worshiping a multitude of Hindu gods. Taking a look at the entire world, we can see that over 5 of the 6 billion people believe in God or gods. This is strong evidence that it is within the nature of people to orient their lives toward a being greater than themselves.

The atheist may object to this, but they are standing in the face of over 5 billion people who give time, energy, and money to the pursuit of God or gods. If we discovered 5 billion people engaged in any other activity, we would immediately conclude that there must be a cause. For example, if one day 5 billion people started to do something as bizarre as painting their faces green, we would wonder what it was that is causing them to engage in such behavior. We would know there had to be a reason. Perhaps the atheist does not have a desire to pursue God, but the vast majority of humanity demonstrates by their actions that they do have some driving force causing them to pursue a divine being.

We have further evidence of this innate inner drive when we consider the satisfaction people experience when they do orient their lives toward God. Augustine noted this in the prayer opening Book I of his *Confessions,* "You made us for yourself, and our heart is restless until it finds rest in you." Just like a baby comes to rest when its mother responds to his or her cry, so also millions of people have experienced a rest as a result of seeking God.

The atheist may challenge this idea also. Indeed, the atheist may never have tasted this satisfaction or rest. But one look at humanity reveals that billions of people are getting enough out of their pursuit of God or gods to continue. They are experiencing some satisfaction or reward.

This experience of satisfaction or reward has tremendous implications. It means that *people can sense God.*

This is part of the worldview of those who wrote the Bible. There are references to spiritual eyes and ears, along with implications that there are other abilities to sense what is happening in the spiritual realm. Because Westerners have the assumption of an insurmountable wall between the spiritual and natural realms, they have difficulty conceiving of how a person in the natural world can receive information from the spiritual world. On the other hand, if a person has a worldview without that wall, it is much easier to conceive of people having the ability to sense things going on the invisible realm.

Some spiritual sensations are demonstrable to those who have not by definition excluded God from the realm of experience. Consider again Augustine's prayer: "You made us for yourself, and our heart is restless until it finds rest in you." Millions of people today will testify to experiencing this rest as a result of making contact with God. Their sense of rest is an experience. It is a sensation. It is a response to something.

The skeptic may object and say that any sensation that is experienced is nothing more than biochemical and neurological reactions in the physical body. Indeed, that may be true, but that is no reason to ignore the related sensations. We can say the same things about the five physical senses. They are no more than biochemical and neurological reactions—yet, we consider them to be valid ways of receiving information.

What experience does a person have when information comes into and through their spiritual senses? That question is difficult to answer. It is much like explaining to a blind person what the sensation of sight is like or to a deaf person what the sensation of hearing is like. Information comes. Other than studying and explaining the physiological changes that occur, it is difficult to explain what the experience of a sensation is.

Yet, millions of people will testify to being able to experience God. They found a rest. They can say, "It is well with my soul." Not only have they experienced a rest as result of making contact with God, but they will tell others of how they sense the leading of God. As we discussed earlier (Chapter 23), God influences this world through His Spirit interacting with humanity. That interaction can be sensed. In fact, that sensation is so real to some people that they have dedicated themselves to mystical lifestyles, with the goal of experiencing God on a consistent basis.

To people who have experienced God, the historical philosophical arguments concerning the existence of God are ludicrous. While philosophers have spent over 2,000 years trying to prove the existence of

God and in the last 300 years most have agreed that God's existence cannot be proven, people all over the world have been communicating with, sensing, and knowing that same God who cannot be proven to the atheistic philosopher.

The point is that people can know God. They have senses that bring in information about God. This is an element of the biblical worldview.

	View of Reformed Theology	View of the Enlightenment	Christianity Separate from W. Worldview
I. God	In Control	Not Involved, Unproveable, Unknowable	Exists, Existence Obvious, Living, Good, Selectively Involved, Sent/Raised Jesus
II. Humanity	Inherently Evil	Inherently Good	In God's Image, God-Awareness, Can Sense God, Can Know God
III. World	Corrupt in Its Fallen State	Wonderful in Its Natural State	
IV. Society	Deteriorating	Advancing	

Anyone who has experienced God has met Him. Those who spend time with God know Him. This is the most fundamental message of Christianity. You and I can know God.

Discussion Questions

1. If indeed there is no wall of separation between the spiritual and natural worlds, how is it for human beings? Is there a wall separating our spiritual and natural natures?

2. Are you conscious of God's presence? Can you sense Him?

Chapter 29

FAITH IS THE EVIDENCE

N OW THAT WE have identified humanity's ability to sense spiritual things, we can bring more to light in our understanding of faith.

I explained in Section I, Chapter 9, that the modern Western person tends to see faith as a blind leap and defines faith as accepting religious ideas for which a person has no proof. This definition of faith is the result of trying to understand biblical truth through the spiritual/natural division. Western people try to establish this understanding by quoting Hebrews 11:1, where we are told that faith is:

> ...the substance of things hoped for, the evidence of things not seen (Hebrews 11:1 KJV).

People with a Western mind tend to focus on the writer's phrase, *"things not seen."* Hence, they conclude that to have faith is to embrace some idea that cannot be seen or, in other words, an idea for which one has no proof.

It is true that the things of faith cannot be seen with the physical eyes, but the writer of Hebrews first stated that faith is the *"substance"* and *"evidence."* To understand faith, we must first focus on this substance and evidence.

Paul went on to explain how many great leaders obtained faith *"when they obtained a witness"* (see Heb. 11:4-5). They each received faith when they sensed God speak to them. They obtained the evidence by receiving within their heart the promise of God. Yes, there must be substance come from God into the heart of the person. Only when a person senses that substance do they have true faith.

Faith Is Substance

The apostle Paul explained faith in similar terms. He wrote:

...faith comes by hearing...(Romans 10:17).

Faith does not come by blindly accepting unprovable ideas. A person must "hear." Paul further explained that a person must hear the Word of God (see Rom. 10:17). Therefore, people should preach the Word of God, but there is no faith until it has been heard within the heart, for as Paul said, *"with the heart a person believes"* (Rom. 10:10).

Let me compare this to hearing a cricket that is making a sound, but you cannot see the cricket because it is hidden. When you hear the sound of the cricket, you have evidence of the cricket. The sound is the evidence of the cricket that you cannot see.

Your heart can "hear" God. If you hear God, you have evidence of God. Again, I say that faith is the evidence. If there is no evidence, then there is no faith. If a person has not sensed the evidence, then he has not received faith.

What is the experience of sensing faith? It is a sensation of assurance. It is a knowing. Just as the sensations of touch or sight are the results of directly receiving information about the natural realm, there is a sensing of faith that results from directly receiving information from God.

We could have a similar discussion about love. It is a sensation, yet it is invisible. It is real and it can be sensed. Just as love is real, so also is faith.

With this understanding of faith we can easily see the error of the Western mind that sees faith as a blind leap and defines faith as accepting religious ideas for which a person has no proof. Quite to the contrary, faith is evidence. Faith is the substance. Faith is proof like the sound of the cricket is proof of the cricket's presence.

Discussion Questions

1. How would you contrast hope versus faith in God?

2. Can you give personal examples of experiencing faith in an area of your life that previously held no faith?

3. Has your faith developed, expanded, and strengthened over the course of your life? If so, how?

4. What works against your faith? What weakens it? Destroys it? Is the destruction of faith always a bad thing?

Chapter 30

THE BODY AND SOUL FULLY INTEGRATED

CONTINUING OUR DISCUSSION on the nature of humanity, now let's consider the nature of the human body and soul.

The ancient Greek philosophers believed that a person has both a body and a soul; however, they considered the natural world insignificant, and being consistent with this, they saw the body as an insignificant container for the soul. Plato compared the physical body to a tomb from which the soul will someday escape to arise into true life. The Hellenized Jewish philosopher, Philo (circa 10 B.C.-A.D. 50), echoed Plato's ideas writing that the soul is a prisoner sentenced to confinement in the body until death.

Ancient Greek Philosophical Concept of Humanity

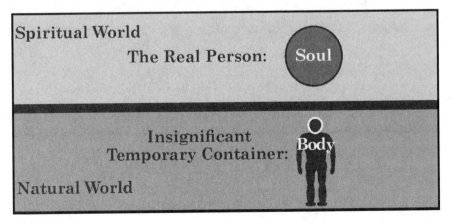

Seeing the soul as the real person, Aristotle defined the soul as the intellect, will, and appetites. By defining the soul in this way, he was assigning to the soul all of the core functions of what it means to be human. In other words, by definition, Aristotle saw the invisible soul as the real person.

Christians with a Western worldview are not as critical of the body, but they are still profoundly influenced by Aristotle's view of human nature. They typically think of the soul as a separate entity from the body, and they will say that the soul of a person consists of the mind, the will, and the emotions. Although they have changed Aristotle's intellect to mind and his appetites to emotions, they are still assigning all of the core functions of a person to the soul. Hence, they are agreeing with Aristotle that the invisible soul is the real person. Although Western Christians would not say that the body is insignificant, they tend to see it as a temporary container.

Western Christian's Concept of Humanity

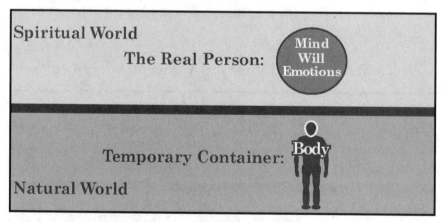

Not all modern Christians have such a simplistic understanding of human nature. Some assign more value to the physical body, and some make a distinction between the soul and the spirit. I will not be making that distinction in this book, but for those interested in understanding the difference between the soul and the spirit see another book I have written entitled *The Spiritual, the Mystical and the Supernatural.* Here I will only identify the spirit as "the spark of life," "the divine life force," or "the breath of God," which God has released into humanity. Setting aside that distinction between the spirit and soul, I will go on to only speak of the invisible soul and the physical body.

The concept that the soul is the mind, will, and emotions is so deeply seated in the thinking of most Western Christians that it is difficult to challenge successfully. Yet, it is nowhere in Scripture. It is simply Aristotle's understanding of human nature inserted into Christian doctrine. To develop a biblical view we must begin by erasing the line between spiritual and the natural realms.

The Ancient Hebrew and Biblical Foundation

S
p
i
r
i
t
u
a
l

N
a
t
u
r
a
l

Second, we must see the spiritual and physical aspects of our being as fully integrated.

To see this, consider a person's emotions. Contrary to what Aristotle taught, emotions are not limited to the soul of a person. When a person experiences emotional changes, those changes are evident in the physical body. They can even be measured with certain medical instruments sensitive to changes in the bloodstream or nervous system. Yes, the body shows emotional responses with various physiological changes and biochemical reactions.

This feature of a person's emotional existence is even more interesting when we consider certain physical stimuli on the human body. For example, when depressant drugs are injected into the bloodstream of an individual, that person is influenced throughout his or her entire being, body and soul. There are certain drugs that can calm a person's emotions, and others that can arouse emotions. Even electrical impulses on certain parts of the nervous system can trigger emotional responses.

What happens in the physical body of a person influences the emotions of that person. Therefore, we cannot limit our understanding of emotions to the soul. Emotions permeate the body and soul.

Emotions Permeate Soul and Body

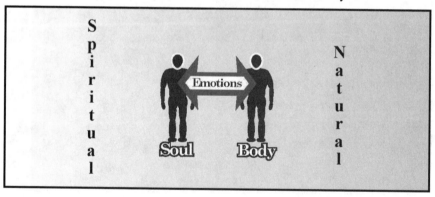

Next, consider the mind and all of the thought processes of a person. Your physical brain processes information, makes decisions, and sends millions of electrical impulses coursing through your nervous system throughout each day. Your brain decides how warm to keep your body, how much food to digest, where to send more blood, etc. Millions of thoughts are processed every minute.

The Body and Soul Fully Integrated

Physical processes correlate with what is going on in the soul. An excellent example of this correlation is Clive, a 66-year-old man who has completely lost the ability to form new memories because of a viral infection that destroyed the related part of his brain. Clive cannot remember what he did five minutes ago. This physical handicap has hindered his conscious life. Hence, we see that Clive's inner being is interdependent upon his physical being.

Again, we see that to develop an accurate understanding of human nature, we cannot divide the spiritual from the natural.

Finally, consider a person's will. Contrary to the Western Christian understanding, the will of a person is not limited to the soul.

To see this, identify the decisions made at the level of the physical body. There are hundreds of biochemical processes going on inside of you right now—breathing, digesting, hormonal release—all governed by the dictates of your physical brain. Of course, you can influence some of the natural processes from a deeper level within your being. For example, you are capable of making a conscious decision right now to stop breathing. In that case, your inner being is ruling over the natural governing processes of your body. However, you cannot hold your breath indefinitely. In just a short time, you will lose consciousness and your physical body will "overrule" your inner being. So your conscious mind has some degree of authority over your body but your physical body has some degree of control over your conscious decisions.

The fact is that many things about your life are decided at the level of your physical body, and you do not have the willpower in your inner person to overpower them.

Decisions made within the body go beyond physical functions. Paul explained that the body is actually involved in moral decisions, and that the body may have within it the desire to sin.

For I joyfully concur with the law of God in the inner man, but I see a different law in the members of my body, waging war against the law of my mind and making me a prisoner of the law of sin which is in my members. Wretched man that I am! Who will set me free from the body of this death? (Romans 7:22-24)

Notice that the will is located in both the inner being and in the body. For example, an alcoholic may have physical cravings for alcohol, and those cravings can be very powerful. In the experience Paul described in the passage above, the will of the body was greater than the will of the inner being. From this we must conclude that the will of a person to sin or not to sin is, in part, located within the physical body.

The main point we can conclude from this discussion is how the mind, will, and emotions are not limited to the soul of a person. Therefore it is wrong to define the soul as the mind, will, and emotions. When I hear Christian teachers making statements along those lines, it frustrates me because I know that concept came from Aristotle and Western philosophy, not the Bible. The human body is more than our container. It is a vital part of our being. Our entire being—body and soul—is fully integrated.

Mind and Will Permeate Body and Soul

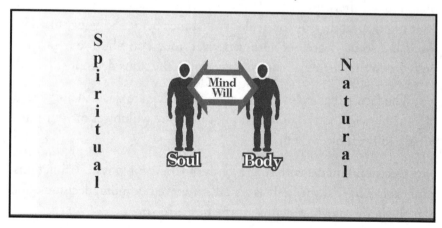

To put this in perspective, consider the incarnation. We are told that *"the Word became flesh, and dwelt among us"* (John 1:14). The Word did not come and dwell in a physical body. No, the Word *became* flesh. Jesus' body was more than a container; it was a part of His being. After His resurrection, the body of Jesus was glorified. Now when we think of Jesus we should envision "Him," not some invisible soul behind His body.

Unlike Jesus, when we die our physical body will decay in the ground. So only in that sense is our body a temporary container. But now while we are alive, our body is a vital part of our being. God created us with a body and without it we would be incomplete. In eternity we will be complete only after we have received new immortal bodies.

A helpful comparison is of an iceberg floating in the water. The top part, which is exposed to the air, is analogous to a person's physical body. The lower portion, which is submerged, is analogous to a person's soul. Now let's say the iceberg floats until it has contact with an island and the bottom becomes lodged there. Then the sun melts away the top part that is exposed; this is analogous to a person dying and their body decaying. But then one day a current comes and dislodges the iceberg so it is pulled away from the island; this is analogous to God calling a person from the dead. When the iceberg is freed from the island it rises in the water and a new portion is exposed above the surface; this is analogous to a person rising from the dead and receiving a new body.

With this comparison we can say that the body is the physical expression of the soul.

Further we can say that the body and soul have similar shape and size. We know this because the Bible tells us in several passages that the soul is in the blood (see Lev. 17:11,14; Gen. 9:4; Deut. 12:23). Wherever the blood is, there is the soul. Therefore, the soul is located where the body is located.

Even after death when the soul is separated from the body, it is still shaped like the physical body. We know this from Scriptures that reveal to us things about the souls of dead people. For example, when Moses appeared on the Mount of Transfiguration, Peter recognized him (see Matt. 17:3-4). When Jesus told about the rich man and Lazarus, He explained how the rich man recognized Lazarus (see Luke 16:23); the rich man even asked if Lazarus could dip his finger in water and cool off his tongue (see Luke 16:24). Such references lead us to believe that the soul has a shape identical to or much like the physical body. What the body has, the soul has. Since the body has hands, the soul has hands. Since the body has a face, the soul has a face. Since the body has a heart, the soul has a heart. Since the body has a liver, the soul has a liver.

It is incorrect to think of the soul as a formless cloud floating in the invisible world. It is more than the mind, will, and emotions. In fact, to fully understand the nature of the soul we must not separate it from the physical body. When God created Adam we are told that God breathed into Adam's physical body and Adam *became a living soul* (Gen. 2:7). The soul was the whole of Adam's being resulting from the life force of God being released into the body. A person is one, functioning as a unit.

The Nature of a Human Being: Soul/Body

There are numerous implications of this understanding, but here I will only mention the following. People who value their physical body are more likely to treasure and take care of it. People who see their body as a temporary, insignificant container are more likely to despise and abuse it.

This is true not only during life, but also after death. Consider how the people in Bible days took care of the bodies of loved ones. They treated dead bodies as sacred, making efforts to carefully bury people where their forefathers were buried. The modern Westerner may read about such caretaking and dismiss it as a meaningless ancient custom. But if we see the spiritual and natural realms as totally integrated then we can see the body and soul as totally integrated. Not only the soul is created in the image of God, but the body is also. The physical body is sacred, and it should be treated accordingly.

People who understand that the soul and body are totally integrated are more likely to live a holistic lifestyle. To be physically healthy, people will realize that they must take care of their inner being. To be healthy within, people will realize that they must take care of their physical body. People with a biblical view see themselves as whole individuals.

	View of Reformed Theology	View of the Enlightenment	Christianity Separate from W. Worldview
I. God	In Control	Not Involved, Unproveable, Unknowable	Exists, Existence Obvious, Living, Good, Selectively Involved, Sent/Raised Jesus
II. Humanity	Inherently Evil	Inherently Good	In God's Image, God-Awareness, Can Sense God, Can Know God, Integrated Body/Soul
III. World	Corrupt in Its Fallen State	Wonderful in Its Natural State	
IV. Society	Deteriorating	Advancing	

Today when you look in the mirror you are seeing you. The real you is not some invisible being behind that face or looking from behind those eyes. Of course, there is an invisible inner portion to your being, but it is most accurate to see your body as *the physical expression of your invisible existence.* This is the biblical view separated from the Western worldview.

Discussion Questions

1. What attitudes toward the body grow out of the idea that the body is merely a container for the true essence of a person?

2. When Jesus approached the multitudes, what was His primary avenue of reaching them? Body, soul, or spirit?

3. How is our approach to God's physical laws affected by our view of the physical body?

4. What is meant by the term "human being"?

Chapter 31

ARE BABIES GOOD OR BAD?

N OW LET'S consider the nature of humanity in the sense of being good or bad. First we will look at babies. (In the two chapters after this one, we will consider adults.)

In Section I, Chapter 5, we discussed Augustine's belief that sin is passed from Adam to all of humanity, and Adam's sin released a moral corruption so devastating that people are born with no ability to resist sin. In this sense, people do not have a free will because they cannot choose to not sin. In Augustine's mind, babies are born totally selfish and are, therefore, totally sinful.

Today when we study the theology of Augustine, we can easily see some of the errors of his reasoning. First, he had a very negative view of sexual passions. Having lived a sexually promiscuous lifestyle before becoming a Christian, he continued for most of his life to be tormented by sexual temptations. Augustine saw passions—and especially sexual passions—as that which tied a person to this corrupt world. This, along with his Greek-based, philosophical worldview led him to conclude that sexual passions are intrinsically evil. In reality, sexual passions are a gift of God meant to be released in marriage.

Second, Augustine considered sexual passions the avenue through which sinfulness is passed from parents to baby. If that were true, then today's babies that are fertilized externally and then implanted in the womb of a mother would be born without that original sinfulness. Certainly Augustine's theology could not deal with this reality that is only evident through modern science.

Third, Augustine was wrong in equating self-oriented behavior with sinfulness. It is true that an infant's behavior is very self-serving because it does cry and act in order to have its own needs and desires met. However, God created an infant with needs and desires. The infant's communication concerning those needs and desires is necessary for survival. Of course, parents should answer the cries of their child with wisdom and redirect some of their child's demands, but the child's communication of its desires and needs is good.

Seeing these truths, we must abandon Augustine's foundational view that self-oriented behavior is sin and babies inherit the sinfulness of their parents through sexual passions.

In approaching this subject, I find many Christians today who are so entrenched in a theology that demands a negative view of babies that they cannot even consider rethinking this issue. Years ago, I was one of those Christians. It was a shaking experience to have my theology challenged on such a fundamental doctrine.

The Scripture that Bible teachers most often use (and I used to use) to teach that babies are born evil is Psalm 51:5:

Behold, I was brought forth in iniquity,
And in sin my mother conceived me.

Teachers with a negative view of humans at birth like to take this verse and apply it to every human being. Yet, studies of the ancient rabbinical writings reveal that King David wrote these words about the circumstances of his own birth. His father, Jesse, had committed adultery, and hence, David was conceived in sin.[1] This is supported by the biblical account of how Samuel came to anoint one of the sons of Jesse to be the next king; Jesse did not even present David along with his other sons because David was not considered a full son (see 1 Sam. 16:1-13). David was the shepherd boy, the isolated son who would not be allowed to get an education or succeed like the other sons of Jesse.

Knowing this about David, we cannot take a verse in which David was speaking about his own conception and apply it to all people everywhere.

So then, we must look elsewhere to develop our understanding of the nature of infants. The best place to look is at the words of Jesus Christ. How did He look at babies and young children?

> *Yes; have you never read, "Out of the mouth of infants and nursing babes You have prepared praise for Yourself"?* (Matthew 21:16b)

> *Truly I say to you, unless you are converted and become like children, you will not enter the kingdom of heaven* (Matthew 18:3).

> *Let the children alone, and do not hinder them from coming to Me; for the kingdom of heaven belongs to such as these* (Matthew 19:13).

The most obvious characteristic that Jesus noted about children is their receptivity and/or innocence.

Christians trained in Reformed theology may object and immediately point out how a two-year-old child may stomp his foot and say, "No!" to his mother. Yet, that same child on another occasion may smile at his mother and say, "Yes." If the child's disobedience means he is inherently evil, then by the same logic his obedience means he is inherently good.

I am not trying to answer the question whether children are inherently good or evil. That is not even the question we should be asking. In developing a Christian worldview separate from the Western worldview, it is just as important that we prioritize truths as we know truths. The most obvious characteristic Jesus noted about children is their innocence. The very fact that Western people want to first decide whether children are inherently good or evil reveals that they are thinking with a Western worldview—in the wrong categories. If we had the same worldview that Jesus had, our first observation would be concerning their innocence.

	View of Reformed Theology	View of the Enlightenment	Christianity Separate from W. Worldview
I. God	In Control	Not Involved, Unproveable, Unknowable	Exists, Existence Obvious, Living, Good, Selectively Involved, Sent/Raised Jesus
II. Humanity	Inherently Evil	Inherently Good	In God's Image, God-Awareness, Can Sense God, Can Know God, Integrated Body/Soul, Babies: Innocence
III. World	Corrupt in Its Fallen State	Wonderful in Its Natural State	
IV. Society	Deteriorating	Advancing	

Further, Jesus implies that children have some spiritual connection with God. Matthew records our Lord's words when He said:

See that you do not despise one of these little ones, for I say you, that their angels in heaven continually see the face of My Father who is in heaven (Matthew 18:10).

Jesus was revealing a truth about children: they have angels assigned to them and those angels have direct access to God. Because of this, we are told not to despise any child. In other words, our attitude toward children should be determined by an awareness of how their angels stand openly before God. Yes, there is a very real association between infants and God's presence.

This idea that babies are not born totally evil or separated from God is not easy to accept for someone who has been raised in Reformed theology or certain branches of Evangelical Christianity. I do not expect to change every reader with the few words presented here. For those interested in further study (including Paul's writings on this subject), consider my book entitled *Precious in His Sight*. For now I will simply say that babies are not as evil as Augustine would have us believe. The most important characteristics of their nature are innocence and connectedness to God.

Discussion Questions

1. What is the relationship between being born innocent and being born good?

2. Were Adam and Eve innocent or good or both?

Chapter 32

ARE PEOPLE GOOD OR BAD?

ENLIGHTENED THINKERS have accepted the idea that people are inherently good. In contrast, the historical Church has held to a very negative view of humanity ever since the time of Augustine.

John Calvin, the father of Reformed theology, taught that people are "totally depraved," or in other words, every part of a person's being is corrupted by sin. Christians who are faithful to Calvin's teachings like to quote the apostle Paul where he wrote, *"nothing good dwells in me..."* (Rom. 7:18). By taking these words out of context, they distort the meaning. Paul goes on to qualify his statement, saying that nothing good dwells in me, *"that is, in my flesh."* The flesh he is speaking of refers to the part of his being that has been corrupted by sin. By definition, nothing good dwells in the flesh. But in the context of Romans 7, Paul is talking about the war going on inside of himself. He explains that the good within is at war with the outer members of his body. This means that there was also good within Paul—if there was no good, then there would be no war. Unfortunately, many Reformed Christians overlook this and cling to a completely negative view of humanity.

For Christians willing to reevaluate their understanding of human nature, the best place to start is not with the theology of Paul (or of Augustine), but with the worldview of Jesus. I cannot overemphasize this point. The Church is supposed to be built on the foundation of the apostles and prophets with Christ Jesus being the cornerstone (see Eph. 2:20). As I have been showing throughout this book, much of Christian thought has been built on the foundation laid by Plato and Aristotle, followed by Augustine. We need a different foundation.

Consider how Jesus viewed people. Several times He referred to good people and bad people. For example, in Matthew 5:45, He said:

...for He causes His sun to rise on the evil and the good, and sends rain on the righteous and the unrighteous.

This assumes that there are both good and evil people in the world. Yet, Jesus was not speaking in terms of Christians versus non-Christians. He was speaking of the whole of humanity—people who had not yet heard the Gospel.

Consider our Lord's words in this passage:

The good man out of his good treasure brings forth what is good... (Matthew 12:35).

The good man to whom Jesus refers did not receive his goodness as a result of a salvation experience. Jesus was talking about people who had never heard of His saving message.

Now, I am not denying that every human sins. Scripture teaches that all people sin and everyone needs the forgiveness available through Jesus Christ. When I speak of good people, I am not saying that they are good in the sense of perfection. The adjective *good* as used in the New Testament is most commonly interpreted from the Greek word *agathos*. This word can mean good in the sense of perfection, or it can be used in a less strict, but still very positive way.

For example, when a certain man came to Jesus and called Him *"Good Teacher,"* Jesus answered:

Why do you call Me good? No one is good except God alone (Mark 10:18).

The goodness spoken of here has to do with perfection—a standard that no human being can attain.

We can see the word *good* (*agathos* in Greek) being used in other passages in a less strict sense, such as in Luke 23:50, which describes Joseph:

And behold, a man named Joseph, who was a member of the Council, a good and righteous man....

The Bible is not contradicting itself when it says in one verse that no one is good, and then in other verses points out certain people who are, indeed, good. Rather, the word good can be used in different ways. Today we use the word good in similar fashion, implying different things at different times and in different contexts. Therefore, we should not be surprised when the Bible says certain people are good, realizing that this does not necessarily mean perfection.

With this understanding, we see how Jesus referred to some people as good and righteous, while He referred to other people as evil and unrighteous. The important point for our discussion is how Jesus used these descriptive terms independently of any Christian experience. Yes, according to Jesus, non-Christians can be good.

We can see biblical evidence of goodness within non-Christians in other passages as well. For example, the description of a Gentile named Cornelius reads this way:

...a devout man, and one who feared God with all his house-hold... (Acts 10:2).

...a righteous and God-fearing man... (Acts 10:22).

At the time these words were spoken, Cornelius was not a Christian. Yet, he is said to be righteous, devout, and fearing God.

The term *righteous* is also used by our Lord when referring to certain people who lived during Old Testament times. For example, when Jesus was rebuking the Pharisees, He blamed them and their forefathers for killing the righteous men and women who previously had been sent by God:

> *...that upon you may fall the guilt of all the righteous blood shed on the earth, from the blood of righteous Abel to the blood of Zechariah...*(Matthew 23:35).

This verse implies that numerous people in the Old Testament times could be considered righteous.

Of course, no one is perfect, and compared with God and in His sight *"no man living is righteous"* (Ps. 143:2). In that sense, only Jesus Christ can be said to be righteous. However, the term *righteous* can also be used in a less strict sense, and we can, as the Bible does, recognize that some people are righteous—not in comparison with God—but indeed, they do have a quality of holiness and uprightness about their lives.

Many individuals in the Old Testament are said to be righteous and/or good: Noah, Josiah, Enoch, Job, and others (see Gen. 5:22; 6:9; 2 Chron. 34:2-3; Job 1:1).

The worldview of the people who wrote the Bible recognized that there were good people and there were bad people. Once again I will state that all people need the forgiveness only available through Jesus Christ. Whether people are good or bad, they need salvation. The main point is that good and bad people exist. Hence, we cannot accept the view of Reformed theology, which says that all people are totally depraved. Nor can we accept the Enlightened view, which says that all people are good. We must embrace the view of Jesus, which recognizes that some people are good and some are bad.

	View of Reformed Theology	View of the Enlightenment	Christianity Separate from W. Worldview
I. God	In Control	Not Involved, Unproveable, Unknowable	Exists, Existence Obvious, Living, Good, Selectively Involved, Sent/Raised Jesus
II. Humanity	Inherently Evil	Inherently Good	In God's Image, God-Awareness, Can Sense God, Can Know God, Integrated Body/Soul, Babies: Innocence, Adults: Some Good, Adults: Some Bad
III. World	Corrupt in Its Fallen State	Wonderful in Its Natural State	
IV. Society	Deteriorating	Advancing	

One more point worth adding here is that even bad people can have some good qualities. Biblical evidence of goodness in non-Christians is in the words of Jesus when He said:

If you love those who love you, what credit is that to you? For even sinners love those who love them (Luke 6:32).

In the context of this passage, Jesus exhorted His followers to love even their enemies. Such love for enemies is divine, but notice also in this verse how Jesus said that sinners love those who love them. Interestingly, the Greek word from which "love" has been translated in this verse is the word *agape,* which refers to an all-consuming, self-sacrificing love. This means even evil people agape love their own children.

In the same passage Jesus went on to say:

If you do good to those who do good to you, what credit is that to you? For even sinners do the same (Luke 6:33).

Here Jesus is exhorting His followers to do good to all people. That is His primary message. But within that exhortation Jesus states that even sinners do some good.

Why am I pointing this out? Because, generally speaking, we can say that there is some good in evil people. This is evidence of the fact that we are all created in God's image. Of course, all people sin and sin has devastating effects on human nature. However, underlying the nature of every person is still the image of God.[1]

Discussion Questions

1. Based on the arguments of this chapter, do you believe that there are non-Christians in the world who are good people? Can these people be Hindus, Muslims, Buddhists, Liberals? Conservatives? If so, how can this be?

2. If there are good people in this world who are not Christians, then why did Jesus give His life and rise from the dead?

Chapter 33

THE HEART IS THE CORE
OF A PERSON'S BEING

THERE IS ONE additional point key to our understanding of human nature from the biblical perspective. It has to do with the very core and governing feature of our being. The Western worldview leads people to think that the mind with all of its intelligence and thought processes is the core of our being. In contrast, the ancient Hebrew worldview recognized the heart as the governing center of a person's being. As the writer of Proverbs said:

Watch over your heart with all diligence, for from it flow the springs of life (Proverbs 4:23).

Where the heart is pointed determines where a person's life will go. A person's future, destiny, relationships, victories, and failures are all determined by where his or her heart is pointed.

If their heart is oriented strongly enough then they will obtain the training, experience, and knowledge necessary to accomplish what they desire. On the other hand, if their heart is timid, filled with doubt, undetermined or undirected, then they will not succeed no matter how much knowledge they possess.

The heart also determines what strengths and weaknesses will be drawn from other people. This is true because wherever the heart is pointed determines to whom a person is bonded. Those to whom we open our heart become anchors for our life. To some degree, their strengths become our strengths and their weaknesses become our weaknesses. We become like the people with whom we associate. Therefore, our heart is a doorway for the character we develop in the future.

Because the heart determines the life of a person, it is more important for a person to develop their heart than it is for them to develop their intellect. This truth is foreign to the Western mind, but central to ancient Hebrew thought.

Further elevating the importance of the heart is the understanding that the heart is what accesses the spiritual realm. With the heart a person senses things in the spiritual realm. With the heart a person believes and anchors his or her life in God.

Finally, we can note that God's Spirit is actively working within the heart of the Christian. The new covenant established through Jesus Christ ensures that each believer will be given a new heart with the desire to please God. Further, God is making His will known by changing the desires within the heart of the Christian.

	View of Reformed Theology	View of the Enlightenment	Christianity Separate from W. Worldview
I. God	In Control	Not Involved, Unproveable, Unknowable	Exists, Existence Obvious, Living, Good, Selectively Involved, Sent/Raised Jesus
II. Humanity	Inherently Evil	Inherently Good	In God's Image, God-Awareness, Can Sense God, Can Know God, Integrated Body/Soul, Babies: Innocence, Adults: Some Good, Adults: Some Bad, Heart Is the Core
III. World	Corrupt in Its Fallen State	Wonderful in Its Natural State	
IV. Society	Deteriorating	Advancing	

The Heart Is the Core of a Person's Being

We will now turn our attention away from the nature of humanity, but this does not mean we have developed a complete picture of human nature. There are innumerable aspects of what it means to be human. We are simply focusing on characteristics that are emphasized by the Bible writers, and we are identifying fundamental aspects that have been distorted because of our Western worldview—in particular, the distortion resulting from the spiritual/natural division at the foundation of Western thought.

Discussion Questions

1. Discuss the ways in which a person can develop their heart. What does it mean to develop your heart?

2. What role does the heart play in accessing the spiritual world?

Chapter 34

HOW WONDERFUL IS THIS WORLD?

THE NEXT CONCEPT to consider in the development of a Christian worldview separated from Western thought is the state of this world in its natural condition. The historical Church has maintained that this world was seriously corrupted as a result of Adam's sin. Because of this, people must struggle to live in this devastated world that is destined for ultimate destruction. At the other extreme is the Enlightened worldview, which leads one to believe that this world is wonderful in its natural state.

Enlightenment thought lays at the foundation of the modern environmental movement. Since the world is wonderful in its natural state, the more people interfere, the more they mess up that which is good. This leads to suspicion of humanity's endeavors at food processing, genetic engineering of crops, modernization of agricultural methods, certain modern medical practices, and CO_2 emissions causing global warming. Advocates talk much about Mother Earth as if she is a very fragile living thing, needing tender care. They also draw on the philosophy of Buddhism and some primitive tribal people groups whose belief systems are founded on the idea that nature is perfect and humanity is best when coming into harmony with nature.

Of course, there are reasons—scientific reasons—why some suspicion should be cast on human interference with natural processes. However, the proponents of the modern environmental movement often go beyond scientific evidence and stimulate concerns based on the philosophical idea that nature is wonderful in its natural state.

Modern Environmental Movement

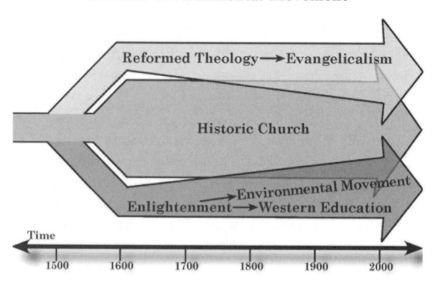

Reformed Theology ➡ Evangelicalism

Historic Church

Environmental Movement
Enlightenment ➡ Western Education

Time
1500   1600   1700   1800   1900   2000

Not everyone in the modern environmental movement holds to the same convictions, but many see Mother Earth as that which created humanity through evolutionary processes. Those same processes created animals, and so, we are not very different from animals. One outworking of this idea is that animals have rights similar to people. Furthermore, living in harmony with nature requires gentle submission to nature rather than exercising authority over nature.

Modern vegetarianism is closely associated with this. Of course, not all vegetarians are in agreement with the philosophical ideas of the environmental movement, but for many the concentrated raising and killing of animals is unnatural, and therefore, wrong.

The Modern Environmental Movement Leads One to Live in Harmony With and in Submission to Mother Earth

How should the modern Christian view these things? Is the world wonderful or corrupt in its natural state? How should we relate to the natural world?

God originally created this world good (see Gen. 1:31), and He placed Adam and Eve in the garden to work six days each week (see Gen. 2:15). The fact that they had to work implies that plants did not grow in straight rows by themselves. Weeds did not stay out of the garden without human involvement, and fruit needed to be picked. Further, God instructed humanity to have dominion over the earth in the sense of exerting necessary force, stewarding, and caretaking (see Gen. 1:28). Hence, the biblical worldview leads us to conclude that this world was created good, however, it was designed with a need to be managed by people.

Recognizing the God-created role of humankind to manage things has profound implications. People are supposed to interfere with the natural processes of Mother Nature. In reality she is not our "Mother," in the implied sense of being over us. She needs us to manage her. Further, she is not a she, but an it. If in our endeavor of managing it, we use all of the intelligence, experience, and wisdom we possess, then this world will become a better place.

The Christian Worldview: People Must Manage This World Well and Make It Better

Management
Caretaking
Improvement

This understanding profoundly influences how people see the world around them. People under the Enlightened philosophical worldview (and the modern environmental movement) tend to think that the natural world would be better without human interference. Therefore, a person holding to the Enlightenment worldview will tend to look at an undisturbed forest—especially a rain forest, which is considered our most undisturbed environment—and see that as natural, and therefore, in optimum condition. A Christian with a biblical worldview can see the beauty in an undisturbed forest, but can also look at cultivated farmlands producing an abundance of food for humanity and see that as optimum. Some forests should be set aside for humanity's esthetic enjoyment. Other forests should be set aside for the production of resources for humanity. The entire world must be managed.

These philosophical ideas also form our understanding of humanity's present attempts at genetic engineering. A follower of Enlightenment thought will tend to think that plants in their natural condition cannot be improved upon. Therefore, genetically engineered crops will always be inferior to crops in their natural condition. In contrast, the biblical worldview leads us to understand that God has placed humanity here to take charge, using all of our scientific understanding to make this world a better place. Of course, people may make mistakes as they learn how to genetically engineer certain crops. Yet, it is our God-given responsibility to endeavor to improve this natural world in every way that we can.

Presently there is much scientific progress in the field of plant modification through genetic engineering. There have been tremendous increases in annual yields and increased resistance to harmful insects. Much research is being done to find genetic cures for cancer and certain inherited diseases. There is no doubt that tremendous good will come out of continuing genetic research. However, there are also justifiable concerns about the long-term effects of genetic engineering. The possibilities are so expansive, it is impossible to know what the overall results will be.

The present environmental movement tends to err on the side of caution, not because of scientific evidence, but due to philosophical ideals. This is not to say that the present environmental movement is void of scientific knowledge. It is their passion to protect the environment that motivates them to find scientific evidence. However, their underlying philosophical beliefs do profoundly influence their conclusions.

At the other extreme are Christians who see this world as corrupted and hanging under God's impending judgment. They would tend to abuse our natural resources and take greater risks in developing ways to reap immediate benefits. The theology of the historical Church has tended to lead to these errors.

What view would we hold to if we embraced Christianity separated from the Western worldview? Well, we have to go all the way back to lay biblical truths on the ancient Hebrew/Christian foundation. We cannot think of the natural world separated from the spiritual world. The natural world is not insignificant. It is good, can be made better, and must be managed by people. Our God-given role is to be good caretakers.

However, it is important to note that people can only be effective in managing this earth as they are in right relationship with God. People were created to be in harmony with Him, not with Mother Earth. Humans in relationship with God, our Father, are to manage this earth and enjoy that which it produces.

	View of Reformed Theology	View of the Enlightenment	Christianity Separate from W. Worldview
I. God	In Control	Not Involved, Unproveable, Unknowable	Exists, Existence Obvious, Living, Good, Selectively Involved, Sent/Raised Jesus
II. Humanity	Inherently Evil	Inherently Good	In God's Image, God-Awareness, Can Sense God, Can Know God, Integrated Body/Soul Babies: Innocence Adults: Some Good Adults: Some Bad Heart Is the Core
III. World	Corrupt in Its Fallen State	Wonderful in Its Natural State	Good, Can Be Made Better People Must Manage
IV. Society	Deteriorating	Advancing	

Discussion Questions

1. How has the term "natural" come to mean "good" in our modern society? Is the connotation always justified?

2. What goes further and is stronger: a blessing of God or a curse of God? What evidence is there for your opinion?

3. Discuss your approach to the dichotomous struggle of living with the right balance of personal control and personal freedom.

Chapter 35

MANAGING OURSELVES

A CHRISTIAN WORLDVIEW leads us to believe that we must manage this world. This includes managing ourselves.

To understand this, recall our discussion in Chapter 32 that there is some bad in every good person and some good in every bad person. Since good is within, it should be released. Since bad is within, it should be held in check. A simple example of this is a mother who allows her love for her family to flow out and govern her own behavior toward her family; at the same time, she might have a bad temper that she must wisely manage.

This idea of releasing some natural desires while exercising authority over others is different than both the view of Reformed theology and the view of Enlightenment thought.

Christians who hold to Reformed theology emphasize the wickedness of humanity. If people are totally depraved then they should totally restrict and control whatever comes out from within them. What is natural is bad, and therefore, it must be conquered and put to death. Indeed, a lifestyle consistent with Reformed theology leads one to live a very controlled life. Christians living within Reformed theology may disagree with me concerning this point. They do not see themselves as living under strict rules and regulations. But it is difficult to understand one's own behavior when submerged in it. I am also making this observation about Reformed theology in comparison to Enlightenment thought, which is at the other extreme of control.

Enlightenment thought leads one to believe that this world is wonderful in its natural state, and this includes the belief that people are wonderful (good) in their natural state. Therefore, people should be allowed to be natural. We need to allow people to "be themselves," free of the judgments and controls of others. Enlightened thinkers also believe that they should be allowed to express their natural desires, especially those related to sexual expressions. Such desires are natural and it is unnatural to restrict them—or so the Enlightened person reasons.

The Christian worldview, separated from the Western worldview, leads us to a lifestyle somewhere between the extremes of Reformed thought and Enlightenment thought. We should release some things from within and exercise authority over other elements of our natural being.

Developing a worldview from this foundation is essential, especially in the modern world where many ethical challenges are being raised against Christianity. More specifically, liberal thinkers maintain that there should be great freedom of expression for natural sexual desires. Because this challenge is so strong today, Christians must think through the issues and decide what truth is. If they have been consistent in the development of their Christian worldview, they will have a firm foundation from which they may hold to truth. For this very reason we are forming our worldview. We need a perspective of life that holds us to truth even when we are being bombarded with conflicting views.

It is easy to understand how other people in challenging circumstances should stand, but it is sometimes difficult to see the need for our own stability in the face of challenges. For example, when we think of Christians facing persecution in difficult parts of the world, we honor them and pray that they will be able to hold to their convictions even in the face of torture and imprisonment. We understand how important it is that they have a firm foundation. Yet, when challenges are placed upon us, we too easily abandon our own beliefs. We may not have identified the challenges we face as equally destructive to truth.

As Jesus said, a house built on sand will not stand when trials come; on the other hand, a house built on a rock will stand (see Matt. 7:24-27). Only if we have taken the time to build our house on a rock will we be able to stand in the face of opposition. For this reason it is vital that we have a sound, well-thought-out worldview.

Think again about managing our natural desires. Do not just think of sexual tendencies, but consider all of the other tendencies with which people have to deal. Some people battle alcoholism, many fight depression, and others seem unable to resist gambling. Some people battle various neuroses, and others are consumed with compulsive behaviors. Some of these tendencies have been induced within because of certain situations that people have endured, and others are the result of inherited traits—they are, in a sense, natural. Only when we consider the whole of the human condition do we realize that natural conditions are not automatically good. Some need to be changed, and some that will not change need to be controlled.

How do we know what should be changed or controlled and what should be released? We must look to Jesus. As I discussed earlier (Chapter 26), a day will come when Jesus judges all people according to what they have done. Therefore, what is good is not what is natural, but what He says is good. Furthermore, what He says is bad is bad.

Contrast this basis for ethics with the basis offered by liberal thinkers in the modern environmental movement. Advocates determine what is right and what is wrong based on whether or not some behavior is in harmony with nature. Good people treat animals and the environment with care and gentleness. Evil people are those who disregard environmental concerns.

Also high on the list of great evils (for liberals) is intolerance. This includes intolerance for individuals expressing their sexual desires. On the other hand, liberals themselves are very intolerant of people who think their own religion is the correct religion. To see this more clearly, recall the liberal belief (talked about in Chapter 9) that ideas about God and religion are unprovable and, therefore, unknowable. Because this idea is at the foundation of Enlightenment thought, adherents see anyone who thinks their own religion is better than someone else's as intolerant, or in other words, ignorant, judgmental, and bad.

This book is not about ethics, but I am just revealing the basis for ethics. The modern environmentalist usually considers what is natural as good. In contrast, the Christian should determine his or her ethics based on what Jesus Christ says is right and what He says is wrong, because on judgment day only His ethics will be relevant.

In summary of this chapter, I can say that the bad within people must be dealt with wisely, while the good within should be released and acted upon.

This understanding of life is different than both the Enlightened view and the view of Reformed Christianity. The Enlightened view leads one to take limitations and controls off so that natural desires are released. The Reformed view leads one to place limitations and controls on oneself because that which is naturally within is thought to be evil. The true biblical view is somewhere between these two extremes.

The good news is that God is at work within the Christian, causing that which is within to become better and better. As Paul wrote:

...for it is God who is at work in you, both to will and to work for His good pleasure (Philippians 2:13).

This is a fundamental truth of the new covenant that God established through Jesus Christ: God writes His desires upon the hearts of all who enter into the new covenant (see Heb. 8:10). As the Holy Spirit is allowed to work in the hearts of people, their desires change. A sanctification process is activated. Therefore, the longer individuals walk with God, the more they can live in freedom, allowing that which is within to govern their own behavior. Certainly bad desires from within must be wisely dealt with, but the better the inside becomes, the less the limitations and controls are necessary. Therefore, the Christian life is one of increasing freedom and victory.

Discussion Questions

1. How can you tell when this is out of balance? What are the signs of too much control? Too much freedom?

2. Which of the two extremes—control or freedom—tends toward greater sin?

Chapter 36

SHOULD WE BRING THE GOSPEL TO TRIBAL PEOPLE?

THE ENLIGHTENED WORLDVIEW leads one to believe that people in their primitive, natural state are wonderful and should not be bothered. Modern Enlightened professors often scorn the thought of colonizing, Westernizing, or Christianizing tribal groups still isolated from more advanced societies. Missionaries are sometimes labeled as the destroyers of culture. Students in our secular universities are often taught to envy primitive tribal people, reverence their closeness to nature, and honor their ancient customs. In reality, anyone who has spent extended time with any primitive people group knows that such ideas are mostly foolishness.

Before I go on to explain, I need to redefine what I mean by "Enlightened professor." One or two hundred years ago this label could be appropriately used for a professor who held to the ideals of the Enlightenment. However, the historical Enlightenment has come and gone. Enlightenment thinking still lies at the foundation of Western education, but education has gone through the same transitions that the rest of Western society has experienced. In particular, today's higher education is profoundly influenced by the Postmodern worldview. In spite of this, I am still referring to "Enlightened professors" because I do not want to point the finger at any certain group of modern professors. By using outdated terminology, I can be as bold and direct as I desire, but hopefully not cause any specific persons to be defensive.

Now returning to the subject of this chapter, I can say that Enlightened professors would have their students believe that primitive tribal people should not be colonized, Westernized, nor Christianized, because those people are better off in their wonderful, natural state.

As a young idealistic student, I may have fallen for that lie, but over the course of more than 20 years traveling around the world, I have come to know better. I have sat around open fires and looked into the eyes of tribal people in six different countries. I have observed, tested, and verified some things about tribal people.

Until I sat with people who have been involved in tribal wars for many generations, I never knew how deeply fears, resentments, and misunderstandings can churn within a person's heart. I never knew how deceived people can be about their neighbors until I met tribal men and women who had never traveled more than 20 miles from the land of their forefathers. I never knew that people could tell so many lies about others until I sat on the mud floors of huts and listened to primitive people tell their stories. I never knew how narrow-minded people could be until I met with people who had never learned to read. I never knew that people could be so mean and selfish until I walked among those who have lived with true poverty and experienced chronic hunger.

To the positive I can say that most tribal people are content. Relatively speaking, their children are happy. Yet, they can only dream about enjoying most of the benefits that more modernized people experience easily every day.

Therefore, when I hear Enlightened professors espouse how we should leave native cultures alone, I wonder which cultural practices it is that they want us to leave intact. Is it their practice of circumcising girls when they turn 13 years old? Or is it the practice of offering up the last of their food to honor the dead, while their children have not eaten a full meal in months? Perhaps the Enlightened professor would have us avoid teaching methods of sanitation so tribal people can continue having an average life expectancy of less than 35 years old. Maybe the cultural practice we should leave untouched is that which allows a man to beat his wife and even discard her because she cannot produce more than four children. Or perhaps it is that cultural experience in which many mothers watch at least half of their children die before age five. Perhaps for the sake of maintaining the dignity of ancient practices we should avoid teaching people how to grow food, cook it, or store it so their children and elderly will not starve during the dry seasons. Or maybe the Enlightened professor would have us leave native men alone so that they will continue believing that AIDS can be cured by having sex with a virgin.

Each time I hear of Enlightened professors holding to their wonderful-in-the-natural-state beliefs, I wonder if they have ever gotten outside of the classroom. I wonder if they have ever looked into the eyes of a woman holding her child who recently died of dysentery that could have been cured with the most common of medicines. I wonder if they know that most native people experience worms crawling out of their anuses. Do they know that primitive people live daily with hopelessness and anguish in their hearts?

I have seen the hardships and negative aspects of tribal life with my own eyes. I have talked with a tribal chief who is killing monitor lizards, which are almost extinct. I have listened to a Christian pastor trying to uproot the lie in the minds of tribal women who believe that their husbands only love them if they beat them. I have met tribal men who believe they will be warriors only by killing a lion with a spear. And I have sat in tribal huts wherein young men are circumcised with a dirty knife, and as a result, up to 20 percent die a painful death due to infection.

Of course, there are some cultural practices evident among primitive groups that should be learned and embraced by modern people. For example, there are often community relationships that are so interdependent and close that modern Western individuals would not know how to act within such dynamics. There is also a humility among most tribal peoples that astounds visitors from an urban society. Indeed, there are some characteristics and attitudes that all of the world should learn from our more simple earth dwellers.

Yet even that can only go so far because it is also true that primitive tribal people typically have very little tolerance for those outside of their own community. They may idolize the rich man who visits them from the other side of the world, but let them talk about the tribe on the other side of the mountain and you will often hear hate like you never knew existed.

Anyone who has built relationships with tribal people also knows how their minds and hearts are filled with superstitions and fears. One tribal chief I know refuses to enter the only nearby river because he believes a demon lives within it. There are still thousands of villages in the world where witch doctors compete for the loyalty of their people and each one is willing to cast a curse on any other person for a gift of a chicken or an armload of corn. In those villages, people constantly wonder if the pains they experience are because their neighbor paid to have them cursed. They wonder which witch doctor caused their sister to bear a child with a deformed leg. They wonder every day if the gods who rule the nearby mountain will demand again that they scourge their body with whips. Their minds are often in turmoil because they are convinced that the ancestors who are buried behind their mud hut are angry and will torment their children in dreams throughout the night. Even this week there will be thousands of men somewhere in the world who will drink themselves into a stupor and lay upon the graves of their ancestors hoping to appease those who are dead.

240

Should We Bring the Gospel to Tribal People?

To someone who has observed the fears and superstitions of tribal people, it seems strange to hear an Enlightened professor declare that we must not bother those who live in such conditions. Part of what makes it strange is that the same professor is the one who will herald the greatness of the Scientific Revolution, which set people in the Middle Ages free of their superstitions. Enlightened professors may herald as great the leaders who broke those bonds of superstition, but at the same time ridicule Christian missionaries who attempt to do likewise to precious humans who suffer today under the weight of superstitions.

What is it that Enlightened professors think Christian missionaries do? Don't they know that it is missionaries, more than any other people, who have brought farming techniques, methods of food storage, medical care, teachings on sanitation, and basic education to tribal people all over the world? Today there are increasing numbers of governmental and humanitarian organizations bringing aid to poverty-stricken areas of the world, but historically it has been Christian missionaries who have established most of the hospitals, orphanages, and schools in places where others have not had the concern nor love to go.

What Enlightened professors actually dislike Christian missionaries doing is bringing to tribal people their "unprovable myths" about God, the resurrection of Jesus Christ, and the future judgment that stands before all humanity.

What is the primary message of the Christian missionary? It is above all else that there is a God who loves people. There is a God who sent His Son to die so that people can have their sins forgiven. There is a God who has power to undo the works of demons and break the curses of witch doctors. There is a God who loves people enough to set them free. And there are people who do have a relationship with God, and hence, those people want to help. I know, because I have met hundreds

241

of missionaries who are helping people in remote villages around the world. They are my friends. It is what we do.

Discussion Questions

1. Thinking back to your impressions of native people before reading this chapter, how have your impressions changed? Where did your original impressions come from, and what formed them?

2. Using the discussion of the conditions of native people as an example, how are we to know when our impressions of any subject are valid or not? How do we know what is true?

Chapter 37

FACING VICIOUS ATTACKS

SOME PEOPLE hate Christianity. Many have written books, produced movies, fabricated documentaries, and propagated lies. They usually believe their own lies. Atheists often accuse religion in general and Christianity specifically as the source of the greatest evils in the world. In his best-selling book *The End of Faith,* atheist Sam Harris declares that religion is "the most potent source of human conflict, past and present."[1] Outspoken atheists like to lump all religions together, throwing the Muslim terrorist into the same category as the average churchgoer. Every few months a new attack on Christianity hits the news and gains the spotlight. Many people act as if they are compelled to discredit Christianity, its leaders, and its values.

As a Christian, it is hard to understand why some people are so antagonistic toward us. Some are hurt and they may have justifiable reasons. Perhaps they were raised in an overbearing, legalistic Christian environment. Some may have observed hypocrisy within church leadership. Some have become convinced of our wickedness because they have been misinformed. Others have listened to offended leaders and then taken on their offenses. There are also some who despise Christianity because of its standards concerning sexual expression. For them to admit that Christianity has anything positive to say would threaten their own lifestyles. It is easier to dismiss the whole Christian message.

When people are determined to reject something or someone, they often exaggerate in their own minds the wickedness of that thing or person. If they are bitter or hateful, their perception is distorted. This is true in all relationships and has been evident throughout history.

It is very evident in the attitudes of atheists and others antagonistic toward Christianity as they make accusations against Christians concerning the atrocities committed throughout Church history. Atheists like to talk about the Crusades, the Inquisition, and the Salem witch trials. They often point out how most of the wars in history have been motivated by religious objectives and led by religious zealots. The wars in Iraq, Ireland, and Israel are offered as examples in modern times. Such discussions are often carried on in university classrooms where liberal professors freely place Christianity in a bad light.

It is true that the Church has made some tragic mistakes and even committed atrocities in the last 2,000 years, but Christians should be able to separate the truth from exaggeration.[2]

First, let's talk about the Crusades of the 11th through 13th centuries when Christians fought Muslims and hundreds of thousands died on both sides. Indeed, the Crusades were tragic. The Church made mistakes and was responsible for some atrocities. The resulting rift between Muslims and Christians is unlikely to mend unless modern Christians admit to the errors of their forefathers. However, as Christians we need not take more than our share of the responsibility. Before the rise of Islam, the Middle East was predominately Christian. Muhammad's armies had been the aggressors, killing hundreds of thousands. Christians were rallied by the pope and responded by trying to take back the regions that had been conquered, and especially Jerusalem, the city that they considered sacred. Most of the Crusades were failures from the Christian perspective, but many historians suspect that Europe would have been totally conquered by Muslims had Christians not risen up to stop their advance.

What about the Inquisition? Those antagonistic toward Christianity love to exaggerate the cruelties and imply that hundreds of thousands were killed. How many were actually killed? In his scholarly work entitled *The Spanish Inquisition,* Henry Kamen estimates the number at 2,000. Other historians estimate between 1,500 and 4,000.[3] Tragic, yes. Catastrophic, no.

Now let's discuss the Salem witch trials. How many were killed? The Salem witch trials were held in 1692, and only 19 were sentenced to death. A few others died in captivity. In total less than 25 died.[4]

Certainly any number put to death was tragic, but to get an accurate understanding of what actually took place we must put ourselves back in those times and culture. As C.S. Lewis pointed out, the people of that time actually believed "that there were people going about who had sold themselves to the devil and received supernatural powers to kill their neighbors or drive them mad or bring bad weather—surely we would all agree that if anyone deserved the death penalty, then these filthy quislings did."[5] The people of the time period were deceived and foolish, but to depict those responsible for the trials as evil is to misunderstand the times and culture.

Today in primitive societies there are still witch doctors being put to death, but we see it primarily as a result of ignorance, rather than evil. In the Congo of Africa, where I have been several times, there are people being accused of using witchcraft even today. Often they are young people. Several hundred have been killed in recent times. But I have never met an atheist in the Congo trying to save their lives. Today it is the Christian Church that has been offering safe haven for the accused, and it is missionaries who are trying to teach the people better ways. Yet, the liberal professor would rather talk about the 19 witches killed by ignorant Christians 300 years ago, than talk about the many being saved and taught in difficult places around the world today.

Next, consider some of the wars during our own lifetime. Although there have been many, the most discussed by atheists include the wars in Iraq, Ireland, and Israel. After all, are these not religious wars?

To think that the war in Iraq was religious is to ignore the fact that Saddam Hussein and his regime were secular and responsible for the deaths of over 1 million of their own people and about 2 million Iranians. Other than the al-Qaeda radicals, the fight in Iraq was primarily ethnic based.

Similarly, in Ireland the battlefront lines may be drawn between Roman Catholics and Protestants, but those lines also follow ethnic lines. There has been hatred between the Southern Irish and the Northern Irish for generations. Having traveled many times in Ireland, I can assure you that the battles between the Protestants and Catholics would be basically the same even if no denomination or religion of any kind were involved.

Concerning the wars in Israel, we need to recognize that the people who established Israel were secular, not religious, Jews. Furthermore, the Palestinian Liberation Organization (PLO) has been secular since its founding. At times, religious vocabulary is thrown back and forth, but leaders throughout history have claimed that God is on their side. It is unclear whether they are actually motivated by religious beliefs or simply rationalizing their own actions by using religious rhetoric.

While stating or implying that religion is the cause of these and other wars, some liberal professors talk as if atheists would never engage in such evils. Yet, let's not forget the atrocities of atheistic communism. Stalin was responsible for about 20 million deaths and Mao Zedong's regime for approximately 70 million. Pol Pot, who led the Communist

Party faction known as the Khmer Rouge, killed over 1.5 million of his own Cambodian people.[6] Add to these numbers the atrocities committed by Soviet dictators like Lenin, Khrushchev, and Brezhnev. Also add atheists like Fidel Castro and Kim Jong-il. All total, atheistic regimes have slaughtered more than 100 million people within the last 100 years. That averages to more than 1 million people per year.[7]

Now bring this picture down to the lives of people in our own communities. People antagonistic to Christianity like to discuss the religious nut who thought he was doing God's will by killing a family member. Indeed, there are such mentally deranged people out there, and they may be paraded on the nightly news. But let's not let that oddity of news blind us from the fact that hundreds of thousands of people who deny God are selling drugs, working in gangs, and killing people on the streets. Very few of them are motivated by religious reasons.

Indeed, we Christians need to admit that there have been atrocities committed in the name of religion. The atheists are correct to some extent. However, rather than see religion as the root cause of those struggles, we need to consider the fact that religion is valuable enough to fight for. By saying this, I am not justifying every religious war. However, throughout the ages, people have fought for money, love, pride, property, to save the lives of others, and for the freedom to govern themselves. In the eyes of the atheist, religion is not as valuable as any of these things. However, through the eyes of many religious people, their beliefs are much more valuable than money, love, pride, property, the lives of others, or the freedom to govern themselves. Religious beliefs are, in fact, of eternal value. Of course, the atheists cannot accept this and they will never think religion is worth risking one's life for. But 5 billion people in the world today are faithful to their religious belief system, and for many, their beliefs are the most valuable things they possess. Rather than condemn those beliefs as the cause of war, we need to consider the fact that beliefs are at times worth fighting and even dying for.

CHRISTIANITY UNSHACKLED

Discussion Questions

1. Is your religion worth fighting for? Worth dying for?

2. Does fighting for your religion always involve physical violence?

3. Does dying for your religion always involve physical death?

Chapter 38

Is Society Advancing or Deteriorating?

WE HAVE DISCUSSED the nature of God, humanity, and the world. Of course, many books could be written to expound on each of these subjects, but in our brief overview, we have identified a few of the foundational points of a Christian worldview separate from Western thought.

There remains one foundational area of inquiry. That area comes to light as we answer the question, "Is society advancing or deteriorating?" In Section I, Chapter 19, we discussed Hegel's view of society's progress through constant struggles. We also discussed the optimism of the Enlightenment and of 19th-century Christianity. That was followed by the skepticism of the 20th century (Chapter 20). While the Western world has shifted back and forth between optimism and pessimism, we should be able to establish our worldview on a more sure foundation than what we see around us. As Christians, we should build our foundation on what we see God doing in the earth.

First, consider God's original plan established and declared to Adam and Eve:

God blessed them; and God said to them, "Be fruitful and multiply, and fill the earth, and subdue it..." (Genesis 1:28).

Christians usually see this as God's command to Adam and Eve. Of course, there is an instructive nature to God's Words, but this is more than a command. We are told that God *blessed* Adam and Eve. In God's blessing and in His Words there is creative power.

To see this, consider how God blessed the animals with similar words: *"Be fruitful and multiply…"* (Gen. 1:22). God was not expecting the animals to respond in the sense of obeying what He said; rather He released creative power with His blessing to cause the animals to be fruitful and multiply. Consider how God said, *"Let there be light,"* and light came into being. When God said, *"Let the earth bring forth vegetation,"* plants came out of the ground. There was enough power in God's words to sustain life and for plants to go on reproducing even unto today. This is how every creative Word of God is fulfilled.

When God said to Adam and Eve: *"Be fruitful, multiply, and subdue the earth,"* He was not merely giving them a command. He was releasing a creative force to cause humanity to be fruitful, to multiply, and to subdue this earth.

The force of God's spoken Word is active even today. As God said through the prophet Isaiah:

> *So will My word be which goes forth from My mouth;*
> *It will not return to Me empty,*
> *Without accomplishing what I desire,*
> *And without succeeding in the matter for which I sent it* (Isaiah 55:11).

The force of God's Words spoken to Adam and Eve is still accomplishing what God desired.

Because of God's spoken Word, there is a force pushing society to advance. Because of this force, people build roads, plant crops, and move mountains. Every generation builds on the accomplishments of the preceding generations. Cities are constructed, forms of transportation are improved, technology is advanced. Society is moving in a direction toward the goal of filling and subduing the earth. This is progress.

Envision this force of progress as a wave originating at the beginning and moving forward through time. Riding the crest of this wave are pioneers, inventors, innovators, and researchers. On the crest of the wave are those who advance society: political leaders pointing the way, songwriters expressing the hearts of people, authors writing books, and artists catching the wind and pointing people forward. Think of people who are driven from within to explore new territories, engineer technological advancements, and discover medical breakthroughs. What motivates these people, often at great personal sacrifice? Of course, people have many reasons for doing what they do, but Christians should also recognize the motivating force of God's spoken Word at creation. It is the blessing of God made manifest.

Unfortunately, many Christians have not recognized this force. They have never been taught about "the original blessing." Instead, their focus has always been on "the original sin." Too many Christians have concluded that the original blessing was deactivated because of the original sin. Of course, we know that sin releases destructive forces in this world, but the power of sin is not greater than the power of God's spoken Word. Even though sinful humanity often moves in directions contrary to the will of God, there is an overriding power moving humanity to advance.

For this reason, we know that medical researchers will find a cure for AIDS. It is only a matter of time before they have a cure for cancer. New forms of energy will be discovered and brought into usage. Governments will progress, becoming better able to handle the affairs of humanity. New problems will also appear because of sin and there will be obvious setbacks, but humanity will continue to advance in the direction of being fruitful, multiplying, and subduing the problems we face.

Humanity Is Advancing

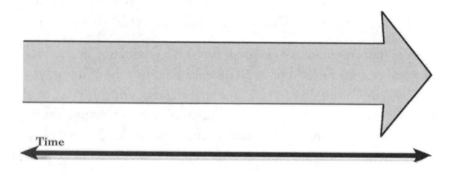

Society is moving ahead and will continue to advance until the day we stand before Jesus Christ at judgment. This concept must be incorporated into our worldview. Progress is inevitable, even unstoppable.

Contrary to what Hegel taught (discussed in Section I, Chapter 19) advancement is not the result of people struggling against each other. Rather advancement is a result of the providence of God. Of course, people do compete and struggle as Ecclesiastes 4:4 says, *"every labor and skill which is done is the result of rivalry between a man and his neighbor."* However, the rivalry between people should be seen not as the ultimate cause of advancement but rather as superimposed upon the inevitable forward movement of humanity.

People Compete as Humanity Is Advancing

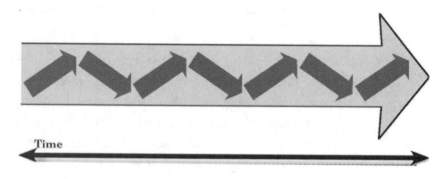

This has profound implications upon our earlier discussion about science being both spiritual and natural (Section I, Chapter 10). If we believe that God's spiritual blessings have consequences in the natural realm, then we will be able to see how His original blessing created a force for the advancement of society. That blessing is not just for Christians, but for all of humanity.

Therefore, scientific advancement is not merely the product of observation and testing. There is an intuitive element. Even a prophetic element. Whoever—be they theist or atheist—catches the wind of God for the next advancement will have God's help in bringing that advancement into natural reality. Because God has breathed His blessings into society, there come moments when society is ready for the next discovery. At the "fullness of times" advancements are made. If one researcher, inventor, or pioneer does not come up with the next step of advancement, some other person will. Hence, our Christian worldview recognizes a spiritual element to natural advancements.

All Advancements, Including the Scientific, Are Spiritual and Natural

If a person recognizes this force, they must give some credit to God for society's advancements—and for one's own accomplishments. We also have more evidence that God is good. This is part of our Christian worldview, separated from the spiritual/natural division.

Finally, we can say that it is one thing to advance technologically, scientifically, and in all of the other fields of human endeavor, but we are answering an entirely different question when we ask, "Are things getting better or worse?" This question we must answer in the final two chapters.

Discussion Questions

1. Do advancements in technology mean we as a society are advancing overall?

2. How do you feel about where we are presently headed as a society?

Chapter 39

THE WILL OF GOD
IS ADVANCING IN THE EARTH

ARE THINGS getting better or worse? In this chapter we will answer this question from the perspective of God's advancing Kingdom. In the next chapter—which is our final chapter—we will answer this question by taking a realistic look at the world around us.

God's will manifests in the earth as His Kingdom manifests. For this reason we pray, *"Thy kingdom come, Thy will be done on earth as it is in heaven...."* Is God's Kingdom advancing? Is His will more evident today in our world than it was in the past?

In Chapter 19, I discussed the advancement of God's Kingdom and how this belief contributed to the Western idea that society is advancing. Allow me to briefly restate that understanding.

Two thousand years ago Jesus walked the earth declaring, *"The kingdom of God is at hand"*—which means it is available and within reach. After Jesus died and was resurrected, He ascended into Heaven and sat down at the right hand of God. When He was enthroned, the Kingdom was established. Today when we submit to His rule, we are walking in and releasing His Kingdom into the world around us.

In several parables Jesus explained how the Kingdom of God is growing like seeds in the earth: first they sprout, then they develop roots, then they push upward, and finally they develop into mature plants (see Mark 4:2-8;26-29). In another parable, He explained how the Kingdom is growing like yeast in dough, little by little, eventually permeating the whole lump of dough (see Matt. 13:33).

The idea that the Kingdom will *"permeate the whole lump"* is key. Jesus was explaining that the Kingdom will extend over the whole earth. In another parable He compared the Kingdom to the smallest seed that grows to be the biggest tree in the garden. At the time of our Lord's return, the Kingdom of God will be the largest most influential entity on earth (see Matt. 13:31-32). However, we still should look for the day when Jesus will return and bring the full force of His Kingdom upon this earth. Therefore, we can say that the Kingdom is here, it is growing, and it will come in power.

This concept is difficult for many Western Christians to understand because of the spiritual/natural division through which everything is viewed. Because there is such a huge separation between the spiritual and the natural realms, they try to force the Kingdom of God into one category or the other. They think that the Kingdom of God must be spiritual or natural, but not both.

Where Is the Kingdom of God?

Spiritual World?

Natural World?

As a result of this division, Christians have vacillated between different views of the Kingdom over the course of the last 2,000 years. The first disciples of Jesus wondered when Jesus was going to set up His Kingdom on earth with Israel as the seat of government (see Acts 1:6). When the Roman Empire began embracing Christianity in the fourth and fifth centuries, many Christians began to have hope that God would use the Roman Empire to establish His physical Kingdom here on earth. During the Middle Ages, the Roman Catholic Church often called herself the Kingdom of God. Equating the Church with the Kingdom is, in part, why the Roman leaders could justify the Crusades in the 10th through 13th centuries—after all Jesus said, *"the violent take it* [the Kingdom of God] *by force"* (Matt. 11:12).

When the Protestant Reformation emerged, leaders like Martin Luther would have nothing to do with the idea that the Kingdom of God was headquartered in Rome. Luther split his understanding of the Church and the Kingdom saying both had authority from God, but the Kingdom of God flowed through the natural governments of this world. One advantage of this way of thinking for Luther was that the German government was then justified in protecting him from persecution of the Church in Rome. One devastating consequence of this division became evident in the 20th century when Hitler committed atrocities against humanity. Because the Church of Germany (the Lutheran Church) believed that the Kingdom of God worked through the government as a separate authority from God, most church leaders did not believe it was right for them to rise and speak against Hitler.

Ever since the Protestant Reformation, there have been large sections of Christianity that have thought of the Kingdom as a place we go to when we die but cannot experience here on earth. Other Protestant groups have attempted to set up their own version of the Kingdom of God on earth. During the 19th century, most Protestant Christians embraced postmillennialism, which says that it is our job to establish the Kingdom of God here on earth now before Jesus returns. During the

20th century, several major Protestant denominations and groups embraced premillennialism, which says that the Kingdom of God is in Heaven right now, but it will come to earth at some point in the future when Jesus comes back.

Christians today continue to wrestle with this idea about what or where the Kingdom of God is. In reality, we cannot answer that question until we uproot the spiritual/natural division at the foundation of our Greek-based worldview. We must see the spiritual and natural realms as totally integrated. What happens in one realm, influences what happens in the other realm. As people submit their lives to King Jesus, it will be demonstrated by their living out God's will for their life in this world. The Kingdom is the reign of Jesus. Where He reigns, His Kingdom manifests. It makes a difference spiritually and naturally.

One place this is evident is in the Gospel of Luke where the disciples went out preaching that the Kingdom of God is at hand; they healed the sick and cast out demons. When they reported these results to Jesus, He said He was watching satan fall from Heaven like lightning (see Luke 10:18). What happened on earth changed things in Heaven.

Similarly, if God subdues demons in the spirit realm, the results will manifest in the natural realm. What happens in Heaven changes things on earth.

Where Is the Kingdom of God?

S p i r i t u a l	**Kingdom of God**	N a t u r a l

Rather than think in terms of the two categories—spiritual and natural—we must think in the categories of obedience or disobedience. When people are obedient to the King, they are walking in the Kingdom. When people are disobedient to the King, they are acting outside of the Kingdom.

With this perspective we can understand Paul's words that the Kingdom of God consists of power (see 1 Cor. 4:20). He also said that it consists of righteousness, peace, and joy in the Holy Spirit (see Rom. 14:17). These qualities of the Kingdom are not just realities existing in the spiritual dimension, but there is power, righteousness, peace, and joy that can be experienced in our lives here on earth.

A schoolteacher who is submitted to Jesus will manifest the Kingdom in her classroom. The carpenter who yields to Jesus is in the Kingdom of God. A bank employee who yields to the leading of the Holy Spirit can experience the peace and joy of the Kingdom every day at any time. The businesswoman who partners with God in her business will bring the King into her business. Whoever is doing the King's will is manifesting the Kingdom.

God is not going to use the government of any certain nation to establish His Kingdom on earth, but any government official who is submitted to Jesus will establish the Kingdom on earth. God is not going to use any army to establish His Kingdom, but individual soldiers who are submitted to King Jesus—no matter which army on earth they are a part of—will experience the Kingdom. God is not going to use any one denomination or Christian group to establish His Kingdom, but all people who are submitted to the King are part of His Kingdom. God is not going to establish His Kingdom in any one location on earth, but it may become more evident in certain areas than in other areas. The point is that wherever people are submitted to Jesus, the Kingdom is in their midst.

Our understanding of the Kingdom of God must not be limited to the spiritual realm, the natural realm, the Church, the government, Heaven, the future, or to any location. The Kingdom is wherever the reign of Jesus is.

With this understanding of the Kingdom of God we can now go back to the truth of how the Kingdom is growing every day. As I mentioned earlier, Jesus compared the Kingdom to a tiny mustard seed that grows to be the biggest tree in the garden. From this we can conclude that the Kingdom of God is to grow to be the biggest entity on earth.

This does not mean that goodness will reign and all evil will be expelled before the return of Jesus. In another parable Jesus explained that an enemy has also come and sown his bad seeds in the earth. Those bad seeds are growing along with the good seeds of the Kingdom. However, when Jesus returns to separate the wheat from the tares, there will be more wheat than tares (see Matt. 13:24-30;37-43). What then should we expect? We should expect to see good and evil continue growing in the earth until the judgment day. But at the time of our Lord's return, the Kingdom will be the most influential entity on earth.

Can this optimistic view be true? What do we actually see happening in the world around us? In the next and final chapter we will take a realistic look at the world.

Discussion Questions

1. Given that the Kingdom of God is anywhere that God is King, where do you see the Kingdom of God growing? Where do you see it diminishing?

2. How can we tell what is truly the Kingdom of God and what is not? What does the Kingdom of God look like? Feel like? Sound like? Act like?

Chapter 40

Is the World Getting Better or Worse?

OUR UNDERSTANDING of the moral and spiritual progress of humanity must first of all be dependent upon our understanding of what God is doing in the earth. This is what we examined in the preceding chapter.

Our understanding is also influenced by our view of human nature. Those who emphasize the wickedness of humanity have no faith for moral and spiritual advancement. They see our condition as hopeless, individually and corporately. In contrast, people who think human nature is basically good, have a more optimistic view believing that society is getting better.

Earlier I offered the view that sees all people as created in the image of God. Because we have a free will, some people become good and others bad, but everyone has faults. With this view we tend to see society's advancement as a struggle between good and evil. When the righteous rise up, good prevails. When the unrighteous rule, evil prevails. This means the moral and spiritual progress of humanity is not only dependent upon what God is doing in the world, but also what people do. The conditions of the earth are very much dependent upon us.

Because of this struggle, we should not think of society's progress as a smooth upward climb. It would be more accurate to envision progress in a sawtooth pattern, but gradually ascending. Society is capable of advancing and regressing, but overall things are improving.

To see this improvement let's lift ourselves to a higher perspective from which we can look over the course of history. We know what life is like today, but let's compare it to the conditions of society in the past.

Start by taking a snapshot of what life was like in the United States 200 years ago. In the early 1800s there were about 5 million people who had immigrated or were descendants of immigrants, but 20 percent of them were slaves. The age of sexual consent in many states was 9 or 10 years old.[1] Abortion was legal throughout most of the 19th century, and records tell us that over one fifth of all pregnancies were aborted, with Michigan having the highest rate at 34 percent.[2] Prostitution in New York City was commonplace with approximately one prostitute for every 64 men; the mayor of Savannah estimated that his city had one for every 39.[3] The percentage of Americans going to church was about equal to what it is today: 30-45 percent.[4] Thousands of people were moving out West and most of them had no churches to attend until years after they had settled and communities had been developed. Tens of thousands of Native Americans were being murdered or forced off of their lands. Thousands of Chinese people were being brought in to serve as forced laborers. When gold was discovered in various regions of the West, gold rushes occurred, which produced some of the most vile and dangerous communities in the world. Many people in the West carried guns for protection because murder was commonplace. Throughout the United States women could not vote and men could legally beat their wives so long as they did not maim or kill them. Alcoholism was at a much higher incidence than it is today. Things in the United States were not better morally, ethically, or spiritually.

Of course, there were some godly individuals laying the foundations of the U.S. government, but the moral and ethical climate of

America was much worse than it is today. The good ol' days were not so good.

Let's go back even further in time to take a snapshot of the whole world 2,000 years ago when Jesus was a child. The Roman Empire dominated civilization and centered around Europe, the Middle East, and Northern Africa. In Italy, approximately 40 percent of the population consisted of slaves. Throughout the Empire, homosexuality was commonplace, especially between masters and slaves. Infanticide was usually practiced on the deformed and weak; sometimes it was practiced for no other reason than the child being female.[5] Most of the Roman and Greek people worshiped many gods such as Jupiter, Juno, and Neptune. Human beings were routinely tortured to death or mauled by wild animals in the Roman gladiatorial arenas. The greatest thinkers of the times thought there was nothing wrong with these practices. Ernest Hampden Cook wrote in his book *The Christ Has Come:*

> The fact is that bad as the world still is, yet morally it is vastly better than it was when Jesus was born in Bethlehem of Judea.... Few people in these days have an adequate conception of the misery and degradation which were then the common lot of almost all mankind, owing to the monstrous wickedness of the times, to continual war, to the cruelties of political despotism, and of everywhere-prevailing slavery.[6]

Outside of the Roman Empire, people in Africa, Asia, and Australia worshiped nature, demons, and their own dead ancestors. Here in North America, tribes had many forms of worship, but no one had a revelation of the Messiah. In South America, millions worshiped a bloodthirsty god who demanded tens of thousands of human sacrifices.

When Jesus came to the earth, there was only one tiny nation located in the Middle East that had a revelation of the one true God, and even its citizens were living in a time of great doubt. All of the rest of the world was lost in darkness. As the apostle Paul wrote:

> ...*formerly you, the Gentiles...were at that time separated from Christ...having no hope and without God in the world* (Ephesians 2:11-12).

That was the condition of the world 2,000 years ago.

Now think of how blessed the world is today. The Gospel is being preached in every corner of the earth. Christianity is exploding in growth across the world, with more than 200,000 people becoming born-again Christians every day. In China there are more than 20,000 per day becoming Christian and in South America there are 35,000 per day. In total there are more than a million people per week becoming Christians.

The tiny seed that came into the earth in that little nation of Israel has grown to permeate the earth. Christianity is, in fact, the largest, most influential force of humanity in the world today.

Are things getting better? Yes, they are.[7]

Still, we should not envision a utopia around the corner. Until Jesus returns there will be a struggle between righteousness and unrighteousness. There may be many difficult times ahead, and under conditions of war, hunger, disease, and lack, people can sink to beastlike levels. Recognizing that human nature is frail and subject to many defects, we must not embrace a Pollyannaish view of our future.

Yet, we can be assured that the world is getting better morally, ethically, and spiritually. Of course, Christians must stay vigilant, and we have much work ahead of us, but we must not lose sight of the fact that we are gaining ground. The Kingdom of God is advancing and Jesus

Christ is Lord. From this we can conclude that the Christian worldview should be a realistic, optimistic worldview.[8]

	View of Reformed Theology	View of the Enlightenment	Christianity Separate from W. Worldview
I. God	In Control	Not Involved, Unproveable, Unknowable	Exists, Existence Obvious, Living, Good, Selectively Involved, Sent/Raised Jesus
II. Humanity	Inherently Evil	Inherently Good	In God's Image, God-Awareness, Can Sense God, Can Know God, Integrated Body/Soul Babies: Innocence, Adults: Some Good, Adults: Some Bad, Heart Is the Core
III. World	Corrupt in Its Fallen State	Wonderful in Its Natural State	Good, Can Be Made Better People Must Manage
IV. Society	Deteriorating	Advancing	Advancing, Struggling, Getting Better

Discussion Questions

1. How have the arguments in this book helped to convince you that the world is becoming a better place? That humanity is advancing? That the Kingdom of God is growing? Why or why not?

2. What do you experience in your life to convince you one way or the other concerning the direction the world is heading?

CONCLUSION

WE HAVE ENDED with an optimistic worldview. Indeed, when we lift ourselves high in order to look over the entire world and over all of history, we can see that things are advancing and getting better.

However, in the Western world we live in troubling times. One of the most disturbing things for modern Christians is looking at society around us and seeing sexual promiscuity increasing. It was much worse in ancient times, but since the sexual revolution of the 1960s it has been on the rise. With it comes all of the related evils like venereal diseases, abortions, children born out of wedlock, and broken marriages. There is also a tremendous increase in pornography through the Internet that was never available to previous generations.

Sad as these evils are, the greater threat to Christianity is the Western intellectualism that we have studied throughout this book. It was not sexual promiscuity that swept across the Christian continent of Europe and left cathedrals empty and people concluding that the Bible has nothing relevant to say to modern society. It was rationalism. It was liberal theology. It was a worldview that pushed God, faith, and religion off to a distant spiritual world. It was a worldview that was taught in our educational systems.

CHRISTIANITY UNSHACKLED

That same Western intellectualism is seizing the minds of people in North America leaving death in its wake. It is also spreading from out of the West to whomever will buy our movies, Big Macs, and blue jeans.

Most Christians are not aware of this silent killer. Instead, they fear the sexual depravity broadcast through our modern media or the rise of Islam. Others think the greatest threat is nuclear bombs in the hands of our enemies. In reality, none of these would be increasing so quickly if people had a solid worldview founded in truth.

The younger generation resists the truths that the Church offers because they are being grounded in a very different worldview at schools five days a week. As children, they are usually taught by well-meaning and even loving teachers who labor faithfully within our educational systems not fully aware of the philosophy behind much of what they teach. When they are older and go off to universities, the teachers and professors they sit under are usually much more conscious of how they are remolding the minds of their students.

But we must not lay the blame on someone else's doorstep. The message that the Church has been offering to the next generation is in many ways Platonic in origin and wrong. We tell our children that God is in control, but they can see on the television news every night that the world is out of control. We tell them that their non-Christian friends are totally depraved, but they know their friends better than we do and they are convinced that Michael and Jessica are not that evil. They hear the preacher tell of impending judgment and how this present world will soon be destroyed, while at the same time their favorite teacher tells them the importance of recycling their waste so we can pass on a wonderful earth to future generations. They may give assent to what we say while living under our roof, but they will be listening to influential and charismatic leaders once they move out on their own.

Conclusion

If I have one thing to offer, it is a well-thought-out Christian world-view. You may have additions to make and even adjustments that need to be made to fit your own understanding of truth. But please establish the foundations of your worldview and share them with the people you love.

Below is a brief summary of the key points in rebuilding a Christian worldview separate from the Western worldview:

1. There is a God whose existence is obvious. God has given all of the world evidence of His goodness. Millions of people have proof of God's existence through the personal experiences they have had with God. People can experience, sense, and know God.

2. God is not controlling, but He is selectively involved in this world. The natural world operates according to natural laws, but God influences this world through sovereign interventions, answers to prayer, relationships with people, deposits of His Spirit, and spiritual laws. Since God can intervene, miracles can and do happen.

3. Jesus Christ rose from the dead and the witnesses to His resurrection are credible. This means:

   • we have proof that God is alive and that He can work miracles;

   • there is a future judgment day coming when we will all stand before Jesus Christ and give an account for what we have done;

   • since Jesus is the final Judge, He determines what is right and wrong; hence, we have a standard for ethics.

4. All people are created in the image of God with an innate awareness of God. The most obvious characteristic of new-borns is innocence. Concerning adults, there are some good people and some bad people. However, both good and bad people need Jesus Christ.

5. The natural world is good, but it can be made better and it needs to be managed by humans in relationship with God.

6. Management of this world includes managing ourselves. As Christians walk with God, their desires become more in line with His desires, and so they can walk in more freedom.

7. Society is progressing, the Kingdom of God is advancing, and even though there is a struggle between righteousness and unrighteousness, this world is becoming a better place.

ENDNOTES

Chapter 5

1. Augustine wrote of his personal sexual struggles in his book entitled *Confessions.*

2. Elaine Pagels, *Adam, Eve, and the Serpent* (New York, NY: Vintage Books, 1988), 129-132.

3. For a more thorough discussion on the nature of humanity, with a more positive view presented, see my book *Precious in His Sight.*

Chapter 6

1. Many modern historians avoid using the term "Dark Ages" because of how negative, and hence, misleading it is.

2. Although our study is focused on the development of Western thought, which is centered in Europe, we would be remiss not to acknowledge the tremendous contributions made by the Arabic-speaking people of Northern Africa and the Middle East, known collectively as the Saracens. During the Dark Ages of Europe the Saracens advanced in many ways beyond their more Northern counterparts. They developed and later contributed to Western society's advancements in mathematics, astronomy, navigation, medicine, and agriculture, along with many inventions and innovations.

Chapter 7

1. The ultimate error of separating the spiritual from the natural is the separation of faith from reason. Luther even said, "Reason is the greatest enemy faith has: it never comes to the aid of spiritual things, but—more frequently than not—struggles against the Divine Word, treating with contempt all that emanates from God" (*Table Talk*, No. 353).

Chapter 8

1. Some historians will go back to Roger Bacon (circa 1214-1292), referring to him as the father of science.

Chapter 9

1. For an excellent discussion on this topic, see Benjamin Wiker, *Moral Darwinism: How We Became Hedonists* (Downers Grove, IL: Inter-Varsity Press, 2002).

2. Cited in Francis Collins, *The Language of God* (New York: Free Press, 2006), 5.

3. Ibid., 4.

4. Ibid.

5. Sam Harris, *The End of Faith* (New York: W.W. Norton & Company, 2005), 23.

Chapter 10

1. This discussion was inspired by and is developed further in Dinesh D'Souza, *What's So Great About Christianity* (Washington, DC: Regnery Publishers, 2007), 83-85.

2. See Dean H. Kenyon and Gary Steinman, *Biochemical Predestination* (New York: McGraw-Hill, 1969).

3. Lee Strobel, *The Case for a Creator* (Grand Rapids, MI: Zondervan, 2004), 77.

Chapter 12

1. I have not established if the Stuff Creator is a he, she, or it, but I will use the pronouns "He" and "Him" simply to communicate more succinctly.

2. Cited in David Marshall, *The Truth Behind the New Atheism* (Eugene, OR: Harvest House Publishers, 2007), 23-24.

Chapter 15

1. One of the most influential programs promoting this way of thinking in liberal churches and among the public today is called *The Jesus Seminar.*

2. On current television, both the *National Geographic Channel* and *The History Channel* strongly promote liberal thought when they address subjects pertaining to Jesus or the corresponding period in history.

Chapter 16

1. For an excellent discussion on the difference between the Gospels and mythology, see Dr. Gregory Boyd and Edward Boyd, *Letters From a Skeptic* (Colorado Springs, CO: Cook Communications Ministries, 2004), 79-86.

2. A set of DVD teachings on this and related subjects can be found in *The Real Jesus,* a scholarly work edited by Jay Rogers and produced by the *Apologetics Group.* For information, see www.forerunner.com or www.theapologeticsgroup.com.

Chapter 18

1. For this discussion to follow, I have borrowed much from two sources: Dinesh D'Souza, *What's So Great About God* (Washington, DC: Regnery Publishers, 2007), 91-111; and Francis Collins, *The Language of God* (New York: Free Press, 2006), 1-158.

2. Both cited in Dinesh D'Souza, *What's So Great About Christianity* (Washington, DC: Regnery Publishers, 2007), 101.

3. John Gribbin, *Science, A History* (New York: The Penguin Press, 2002), 9-19, 47-56.

4. This discussion about Galileo is taken from and more thoroughly presented in Dinesh D'Souza, *What's So Great About Christianity* (Washington, DC: Regnery Publishers, 2007), 106-110; see also, John Gribbin, *Science, A History* (New York: The Penguin Press, 2002), 95-101.

5. Dinesh D'Souza, *What's So Great About Christianity* (Washington, DC: Regnery Publishers, 2007), 110.

6. One other person who is sometimes portrayed as a scientist who was persecuted by the Church is Giordano Bruno (A.D. 1548-1600). He was a supporter of Copernicus and was burned to death, but he was condemned because of his heretical ideas related to the Trinity, not his scientific beliefs. See Dinesh D'Souza, *What's So Great About Christianity* (Washington, DC: Regnery Publishers, 2007), 104; and John Gribbin, *Science, A History* (New York: The Penguin Press, 2002), 17.

7. Dinesh D'Souza, *What's So Great About Christianity* (Washington, DC: Regnery Publishers, 2007), 97.

8. In particular, Christian Fundamentalism, which emerged from Evangelical Christianity in the early 1900s, continues to reject the theory of evolution.

9. Examples of this include the decree issued in 1992 by Pope John Paul II apologizing for the Church's judgment of Galileo; Pope John Paul II's support of theistic evolution in 1996; and the Roman Catholic Church officially pronouncing in 1951 that the big bang theory model is in accordance with the Bible.

10. One of several organizations dedicated to synchronizing faith and science is the *American Scientific Association,* which has several thousand members who are both Evangelical Christians and scientists. For information, see www.asa3.org.

Chapter 19

1. In ancient Hebrew thought there was also an element of cyclic thought, but only in the sense of connecting the people of all time periods, rather than in the sense of reoccurring events. I have explained this in my book entitled *Who Is God?*

2. For a clearer understanding of this progressive view of the Kingdom of God, see my book entitled *Victorious Eschatology.*

Section II

1. I am firmly in the midst of this group having a Bachelor of Science degree, having studied at three different Western Evangelical seminaries, and presently being a visiting instructor at several Bible colleges.

2. For those interested in a fuller explanation of this, see my book entitled *Who Is God?*

Chapter 21

1. By placing God's existence under the category of Christianity separate from the Western worldview, and not under Reformed theology, I do not mean to imply that all Reformed theologians would

disagree with this. I am simply starting with a clean slate to list the most obvious characteristics that we are led to accept with this view.

Chapter 22

1. As mentioned earlier, I have not established if the Stuff Creator is a he, she, or it, but I will use the pronouns "He" and "Him" simply to communicate more succinctly.

Chapter 24

1. For those interested in further study on this and related subjects, see my book entitled *Who Is God?*

Chapter 25

1. Augustine would say that to accept what others say is "believing," rather than "knowing." In contrast, I am using the terminology, "accept as fact," and I am equating this with knowing when people are confident enough in the information to base personal decisions on what they have accepted as fact.

Chapter 26

1. As atheist-turned-theist, Lee Strobel wrote, "For me, living without God meant living one hundred percent for myself. Freed from someday being held accountable for my actions, I felt unleashed to pursue personal happiness and pleasure at all costs." Lee Strobel, *The Case for a Creator* (Grand Rapids, MI: Zondervan, 2004), 25.

2. Flavius Josephus, *Josephus, The Complete Works.* Translated by William Whiston (Nashville, TN: Thomas Nelson Publishers, 1998), The Antiquities of the Jews, xviii:iii:2.

3. Tacitus, *Annuals* XV. 44. The Oxford Translation, Revised (New York: Harper and Brothers, 1858), 423.

4. Pliny, *Letters* X.xcvi. Loeb Classical Library. English translation by William Melmoth, revised by W.M.L. Hutchinson (London: William Heinemann; Cambridge, MA: Harvard University Press, 1935), II, 403.

5. Suetonius, *The Lives of the Caesars, Nero* XVI. Loeb Classical Library, English translation by J.C. Rolfe (London: William Heinemann; New York: G.P. Putnam's Sons), II, 111.

6. Lucian, *The Passing of Peregrinus* 12-13, Loeb Classical Library. English translation by A.M. Harmon (London: William Heinemann, Ltd.; Cambridge, MA: Harvard University Press, 1936), 13, 15.

7. It is possible that Luke never actually saw the resurrected Lord, but he started his Gospel explaining that he fully investigated the issues having talked to the eyewitnesses.

Chapter 28

1. Teachers of Reformed theology would agree that people are created in the image of God, but it is not their primary point. They prefer to emphasize how all people are sinners and fallen because of Adam's sin.

Chapter 31

1. *Elliot's Commentary on the Whole Bible,* Vol. IV (Grand Rapids, MI: Zondervan, 1981), 61.

Chapter 32

1. This truth is expressed beautifully in Harry R. Boer's book, *An Ember Still Glowing* (Grand Rapids, MI: Eerdmans Publishing Co., 1990).

Chapter 37

1. Sam Harris, *The End of Faith* (New York: W.W. Norton & Company), 35.

2. The discussion that follows is inspired by and more thoroughly presented in Dinesh D'Souza, *What's So Great About Christianity* (Washington, DC: Regnery Publishers, 2007), 204-221.

3. Ibid., 207.

4. *The World Book Encyclopedia,* Vol. 17 (Chicago, IL: World Book Inc.: 1990), 61; Dinesh D'Souza, *What's So Great About Christianity* (Washington, DC: Regnery Publishers, 2007), 207.

5. C.S. Lewis, *Mere Christianity* (New York: HarperCollins Publishers, 1972), 14.

6. These are very conservative estimates.

7. Dinesh D'Souza, *What's So Great About Christianity* (Washington, DC: Regnery Publishers, 2007), 214.

Chapter 40

1. Stephanie Coontz, *The Way We Never Were: American Families and the Nostalgia Trap* (New York, NY: Basic Books, 1992), 184.

2. Ronald A. Wells, *History Through the Eyes of Faith* (New York, NY: HarperCollins Publishers, 1989), 179.

3. John D'Emilio and Estelle Freedman, *Intimate Matters: A History of Sexuality in America* (New York, NY: Harper and Row, 1988), 65, 133-134.

4. Dean Merrill, *Sinners in the Hands of an Angry Church* (Grand Rapids, MI: Zondervan Publishing, 1997), 96-97; in their book, *The*

Churching of America (pp. 23-23), Roger Finke and Rodney Stark document how church attendance went from 17 percent in 1776 to 37 percent in 1860.

5. Alvin Schmidt, *How Christianity Changed the World* (Grand Rapids, MI: Zondervan, 2004), 49.

6. Cited on www.preteristarchive.com/StudyArchive/h/hampden-cook _earnest.html

7. For an excellent book explaining and giving statistical data on how things are getting better, see Stephen Moore and Julian Simon, *It's Getting Better All the Time* (Washington, DC: Cato Institute, 2000).

8. For those who are interested in further study on this optimistic view, see my book entitled *Victorious Eschatology.*

RECOMMENDED READING ON RELATED SUBJECTS

Boyd, Gregory and Edward Boyd. *Letters From a Skeptic.* Colorado Springs, CO: Cook Communications Ministries, 2004.

Collins, Francis. *The Language of God.* New York: Free Press, 2006.

D'Souza, Dinesh. *What's So Great About Christianity.* Washington, DC: Regnery Publishers, 2007.

Finke, Roger and Rodney Stark. *The Churching of America, 1776-2205.* London: Rutgers University Press, 2007.

Gribbin, John. *Science, A History.* New York: The Penguin Press, 2002.

Marshall, David. *The Truth Behind the New Atheism.* Eugene, OR: Harvest House Publishers, 2006.

Moore, Stephen and Julian Simon. *It's Getting Better All the Time.* Washington, DC: Cato Institute, 2000.

Schmidt, Alvin. *How Christianity Changed the World.* Grand Rapids, MI: Zondervan, 2004.

Stark, Rodney. *The Victory of Reason.* New York: Random House, 2006.

Strobel, Lee. *The Case for a Creator.* Grand Rapids, MI: Zondervan, 2004.

Wells, Ronald A. *History Through the Eyes of Faith.* New York: Harper-Collins Publishers, 1989.

Wiker, Benjamin. *Moral Darwinism: How We Became Hedonists.* Downers Grove, IL: InterVarsity Press, 2002.

Other Recommended Books
by Harold R. Eberle

Who Is God?

Challenging the traditional Western view of God, Harold R. Eberle presents God as a Covenant-maker, Lover, and Father. Depending on Scripture, God is shown to be in a vulnerable, open, and cooperative relationship with His people. This book is both unsettling and enlightening—revolutionary to most readers—considered by many to be Harold's most important contribution to the Body of Christ.

Precious In His Sight
A Fresh Look at the Nature of Humanity

During the Fourth Century Augustine taught about the nature of man using as his key Scripture a verse which had been mistranslated. Since that time the Church has embraced a false concept of man which has negatively influenced every area of Christianity. It is time for Christians to come out of darkness! This book has implications upon our understanding of sin, salvation, Who God is, evangelism, and how we can live the daily victorious lifestyle.

Victorious Eschatology
A Partial Preterist View
Co-authored by
Harold R. Eberle and Martin Trench

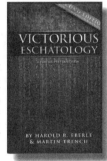

Here it is—a biblically-based, optimistic view of the future. Along with a historical perspective, this book offers a clear understanding of Matthew 24, the book of Revelation, and other key passages about the events to precede the return of Jesus Christ. Satan is not going to take over this world. Jesus Christ is Lord and He will reign until every enemy is put under His feet!

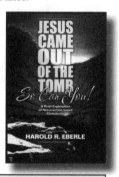